ACCELERATED MCSE STUDY GUIDE

Networking Essentials
Exam 70-058

ACCELERATED MCSE
STUDY GUIDE

Networking Essentials
Exam 70-058

DAVE KINNAMAN

LOUANN BALLEW

McGraw-Hill

New York • San Francisco • Washington, D.C. • Auckland • Bogotá
Caracas • Lisbon • London • Madrid • Mexico City • Milan
Montreal • New Delhi • San Juan • Singapore
Sydney • Tokyo • Toronto

Library of Congress Cataloging-in-Publication Data

Kinnaman, Dave.
    Accelerated MCSE study guide networking essentials / Dave
Kinnaman, LouAnn Ballew.
        p.   cm.
    Includes index.
    ISBN 0-07-067685-2
    1. Electronic data processing personnel—Certification.
2. Microsoft software—Examinations—Study guides.   3. Computer
networks.   I. Ballew, LouAnn.   II. Title.
QA76.3.K56   1999
004.6'076—dc21   98-36279
                                                   CIP

McGraw-Hill

A Division of The McGraw-Hill Companies

1 2 3 4 5 6 7 8 9 0   AGM/AGM   9 0 3 2 1 0 9 8

ISBN 0-07-067685-2

*The sponsoring editor for this book was Michael Sprague and the production supervi-
sor was Pamela Pelton. It was set in Stone Serif by North Market Street Graphics.*

Printed and bound by Quebecor/Martinsburg.

McGraw-Hill books are available at special quantity discounts to use as premi-
ums and sales promotions, or for use in corporate training programs. For more
information, please write to the Director of Special Sales, McGraw-Hill, 11
West 19th Street, New York, NY 10011. Or contact your local bookstore.

CONTENTS

PREFACE

This study guide is designed to provide you with the distilled efforts of expert instructors, authors, and technical professionals who have studied, analyzed, and taught about networking essentials. This study guide provides what you will need to know about the operation and administration of real-world networks to progress toward the MCSE certificate by passing the Networking Essentials exam.

Comprehensive Real-World Networking—Not

Statements of fact, opinions, and explanations given in this study guide are not intended to discourage the exploration of other methods or points of view. In the real world, there are many networking variations that are simply not covered here, because the *examination does not cover everything in the world.*

You *will* find here primarily matters covered in one Microsoft examination. We presume that the reader intimately understands that real-world experience in dealing with the daily upkeep of software and hardware is crucial to success on all MCSE examinations, and to success on the job. As such, this study guide focuses on issues found on one particular examination to the exclusion of some concepts and alternative methods that might be considered vital in one company or in any one networking work setting. Therefore, this guide is a starting point to open the reader to essential concepts and approaches, to fundamental software and hardware ideas, and to assist the reader to absorb the subset of knowledge that appears on the test in question. We have not set out to train *new network technicians* or *world-class network administrators.* Our focus is on one Microsoft examination, exclusively.

Here you will find abundant, clearly worded definitions, explanations, examples, notes, reviews, and summaries that provide exact Microsoft terminology and knowledge and guide you toward real-world experiences necessary to master the exam. You'll also find pointers and references to materials not presented here. Throughout, this study guide provides you with many sources for sample test questions and answers, networking white papers, hardware and software vendors, and other valuable information to prepare you for the exam and becoming an expert networking professional.

MCSE Study Is Not a Snap

Understanding networking essentials and passing the Microsoft Networking Essentials examination is not a snap, regardless of whatever fine preparation materials you own. You wil **not** find the Networking Essentials examination easy unless you actively apply your own powers of perception, acquisition, and memory by engaging and studying what is in this guide and integrating what you know with your own real-world networking experience. As you become actively involved in understanding the material presented in this study guide, you increase your likelihood of passing the examination on your first attempt, and of succeeding in applying your knowledge in the real-world networking environment of the future.

ACKNOWLEDGMENTS

Thanks to Austin Gleeson of the University of Texas at Austin (UT-A), who taught me that computers are programmable, effective tools, and to Robin Eddy, also of UT-A, who taught me to only change one thing at a time! And thanks also to Bill Reynolds, an early graduate from the UT-A Graduate School of Business Information Systems Management MBA program, for encouraging me, way back when, to build my first home computer.

Waterside Productions is lucky to have the services of Margot Maley. Margot's ceaseless enthusiasm and creativity have infused and improved this project in dozens of ways. Once again, although it is inadequate, "Thanks, Margot."

Michael Sprague, whose vision for this project has kept us focused for months at a time, should not be left out. The beautiful layout and attractive style of the book in your hands is very much his creative responsibility, along with Christine Ducker and Jill Lynch of North Market Street Graphics.

We also want to give our heartfelt thanks and warm gratitude to John Mauritz, MCSE+I, MCT, CNE, for writing Chapter 14, "Network Protocols," and to Curt Simmons, MCSE, MCT, for his creative and rapid work with Chapter 17, "Taming the Network," Chapter 18, "Node Addressing," and Chapter 20, "Troubleshooting." Curt Simmons also provided pleasant, speedy technical editorial reviews of this entire book. Theresa Hadden also contributed writing in more than one chapter.

Two good friends who deserve mention are computer maestro David Bauerlein and network maven James Thames. Without comfort, feedback and support from friends like these, I would go astray more often than I do. I also owe a debt of thanks to Johann Pachelbel (1653–1706), for his *Canon in D* for strings and continuo, which helps keep me focused through confusing times.

My thanks also goes to the Texas Workforce Commission, for motivating me to finally leave state employment after 18 years. I'll miss many of my former state worker friends and coworkers, but I cannot avoid the conclusion that state government work has deteriorated perilously in the 1990s and is no longer what it once was. We are also indebted to Herb Martin of LearnQuick .Com for his extravagant study, exceptional attention to detail, and unlimited technical competence.

I also want to take a moment to encourage MCSE candidate and pilot David Bartz, MCP, to hang in there. There is a certificate at the end of the course.

Dave Kinnaman
<kinnaman@world.std.com>

LouAnn Ballew
<ballew@Emissary.Org>

May 1998
Austin, Texas

CHAPTER 1

Introduction

Plan Your MCSE Process

So you want to become a Microsoft Certified Systems Engineer (MCSE) do you? Then you've made a good choice in purchasing this book, because it's specifically designed to prepare you for a vital MCSE examination. And this chapter is designed to prepare you for planning the whole process of becoming an MCSE, and to assist you in outlining the unique process for you to follow to pass all of your MCSE examinations.

According to Microsoft, "Microsoft Certified Systems Engineers design, install, support, and troubleshoot information systems. MCSEs are network gurus, support technicians and operating system experts." That's a central information-technology role with major responsibilities in today's computer networking world.

Preparing for such a major role takes a solid plan. You must know all your options. So, let's begin the planning with a discussion of the components of the objective: the core exams and elective exams that lead toward the MCSE certificate. After identifying the core and elective exams, the remainder of this section is devoted to dispelling several myths about MCSE exams, which could derail your plan if you believed them.

Core and Elective Exams

Two tracks toward the MCSE actually exist at this writing. However, the vast majority of candidates concentrate on the more recent track. The older track is based on Windows NT 3.51, and the newer track is based on Windows NT 4.0. Because the exams for Windows NT 3.51 have been scheduled for retirement, little more will be said about Windows NT 3.51.

Microsoft Windows NT 4.0 Track

This track consists of mastering four core exams and two elective exams. All of the many current elective exams are presented after the core exams.

You must choose 4 core exams from these 8:

- 70-030: Microsoft Windows 3.1 (retires September 1998)
- 70-048: Microsoft Windows for Workgroups 3.11 (retires September 1998)
- 70-058: Networking Essentials
- 70-064: Implementing and Supporting Microsoft Windows 95
- 70-067: Implementing and Supporting Microsoft Windows NT Server 4.0
- 70-068: Implementing and Supporting Microsoft Windows NT Server 4.0 in the Enterprise
- 70-073: Microsoft Windows NT Workstation 4.0
- 70-098: Implementing and Supporting Microsoft Windows 98

You must choose 2 elective exams. There are a great number of elective exams available. You can choose to become expert on any 2 of these 10 software products:

1. SNA Server
2. Systems Management Server
3. SQL Server
4. TCP/IP on Microsoft Windows NT
5. Exchange Server
6. Internet Information Server
7. Proxy Server

8. Microsoft Mail for PC Networks—Enterprise

9. Site Server

10. Explorer 4.0 by Using the Internet Explorer Administration Kit

CAUTION
Microsoft allows you to use, as electives, exams for one, two, or three versions of several software products. Only one exam per product, regardless of version, can be counted toward the two-elective requirement. For example, if you pass both 70-013: Implementing and Supporting Microsoft SNA Server *version 3.0* and 70-085: Implementing and Supporting Microsoft SNA Server *version 4.0,* these two exams will only count for one elective. *The point is that passing exams on two versions of one product won't count as two electives—only one will count as an elective.*

Choose one exam from each of the following products to be counted toward fulfilling your two-elective requirement:

70-013: Implementing and Supporting Microsoft SNA Server 3.0

70-085: Implementing and Supporting Microsoft SNA Server 4.0

Or

70-014: Implementing and Supporting Microsoft Systems Management Server 1.0 (retired)

70-018: Implementing and Supporting Microsoft Systems Management Server 1.2

70-086: Implementing and Supporting Microsoft Systems Management Server 2.0

Or

70-021: Microsoft SQL Server 4.2 Database Implementation

70-027: Implementing a Database Design on Microsoft SQL Server 6.5

70-029: Implementing a Database Design on Microsoft SQL Server 7.0

Or

70-022: Microsoft SQL Server 4.2 Database Administration for Microsoft Windows NT

70-026: System Administration for Microsoft SQL Server 6.5

70-028: System Administration for Microsoft SQL Server 7.0

Or

70-053: Internetworking Microsoft TCP/IP on Microsoft Windows NT (3.5–3.51)

70-059: Internetworking with Microsoft TCP/IP on Microsoft Windows NT 4.0

Or

70-075: Implementing and Supporting Microsoft Exchange Server 4.0 (retired June 1, 1998)*

70-076: Implementing and Supporting Microsoft Exchange Server 5.0

70-081: Implementing and Supporting Microsoft Exchange Server 5.5

Or

70-077: Implementing and Supporting Microsoft Internet Information Server 3.0 and Microsoft Index Server 1.1

70-087: Implementing and Supporting Microsoft Internet Information Server 4.0

Or

70-078: Implementing and Supporting Microsoft Proxy Server 1.0

70-088: Implementing and Supporting Microsoft Proxy Server 2.0

Or

70-037: Microsoft Mail for PC Networks 3.2-Enterprise

---

* If you have already passed elective exam 70-075: for Exchange Server 4.0 you will be required to take a replacement elective exam on or before September 1, 1999. Replacement exams include all current MCSE electives listed here.

Or

70-056: Implementing and Supporting Web Sites Using Microsoft
Site Server 3.0

Or

70-079: Implementing and Supporting Microsoft Internet Explorer
4.0 by Using the Internet Explorer Administration Kit

With all of these options available, MCSE candidates can surely
find elective exams that fit their own career and workplace goals.

Required Software and Hardware

Many current MCSE holders earned their certificates at little or no
out-of-pocket expense to themselves, because their employers
paid the costs for both training and exams. Many of them also did
all or almost all of their exam preparation on the clock, so that
their employers actually paid them to get an MCSE certificate.
These fortunate MCSEs didn't even have to pay for software or
equipment, because their employers also supplied appropriate
software and hardware needed to practice all the skills necessary
for their MCSE exams. If your employer offers this kind of comprehensive support, wonderful. On the other hand, if your
employer expects you to pay your way to the MCSE entirely by
yourself, here are some thoughts on what you'll need.

Required Software

In most cases you'll need at least one copy of both the server and
the client software, because most MCSE exams are about *administering networks* that contain the software in question. You'll need to
know how the product works from both the client and administrator's points of view, even if the exam is specifically about a client
software, such as Windows NT 4.0 Workstation. As just mentioned,
the MCSE exams are usually from the system support and administrator's points of view, rather than the client user's point of view.

Installing a Microsoft client software may, of course, require a
preexisting operating system or a previous version of the client
software, depending on the product involved.

Similarly, several Microsoft server operating systems will
require you to have *other* server operating systems already avail-

able on the network, or installed and underlying on the server computer. This means that more than one server software program may be required for you to use and become familiar with all the tested features of the server software required for the exam.

Minimum Required Hardware

1. One or more Windows NT Workstation computers:

   - 12 MB of RAM.
   - VGA video.
   - Keyboard.
   - IDE, EIDE, SCSI, or ESDI hard disk.
   - 486/25 processor or faster.
   - 124 MB free hard disk drive space (recommended minimum: over 300 MB, including a copy of the entire i386 installation directory [223 MB] plus Windows 95 or MS-DOS 6.22). For hard disk controllers using translation mode to address the drive, increase these minimum sizes by 80 MB.
   - CD-ROM drive, or a floppy disk drive and an active network connection.

2. One or more Windows NT Server computers:

   - 16 MB of RAM (32 MB or more recommended).
   - VGA video.
   - Keyboard.
   - IDE, EIDE, SCSI, or ESDI hard disk.
   - 486/25 processor (486DX2/50 or better preferred).
   - 124 MB free hard disk drive space (recommended minimum: over 300 MB, including a copy of the entire i386 installation directory [223 MB] plus Windows 95 or MS-DOS 6.22). For hard disk controllers using translation mode to address the drive, increase these minimum sizes by 80 MB.
   - CD-ROM drive (Windows NT compatible recommended) or a floppy disk drive and an active network connection.
   - Recommended: 28.8 v. 34 (or faster) external modem, for remote debugging and troubleshooting.

Costs to Obtain an MCSE

As previously mentioned, the costs of an MCSE certificate are invisible to many current certificate holders, because the costs are entirely supported by their employers. Because these advanced skills are of great value to the workplace, it's appropriate that employers provide this support in exchange for more efficient and more productive work skills.

Some supportive employers do require a contract, to assure themselves that the newly trained MCSEs will not change jobs shortly after obtaining their MCSE certificates—presumably before the current employers have had time to recoup the costs of the MCSEs for their former employees. These contracts typically require the employee to repay MCSE costs on a prorated basis, depending on how long the MCSE candidate remained with the former employer. Often the new employer picks up the costs of buying out the former employer's training contract, as a part of the new and more advantageous employment agreement.

Note that MCSE holders are considered more employable and, therefore, more mobile in their employment. The cost efficiency of information-technology workplaces has been hard hit by a mercenary, contract-worker mentality that drains the spirit from workers. In contrast, employers who provide an environment of mutual trust and employment security, by fostering loyalty and goodwill in all employees, will obtain the best return on their investment in employee MCSE training.

MCSE Expense Budget

- Examinations $600 (retests at $100 each)
- Training, seminars, workshops   _____
- Study time   _____
- Books and materials   _____
- Practice examination software   _____
- Network hardware,
  network analysis equipment   _____
- Server and client hardware   _____
- Server and client software   _____

MCSE Myth 1—Everyone Must Take Six Exams to Earn the MCSE

Reality—Some People Are Exempt from One Exam

Some networking professionals are exempt from taking the Networking Essentials exam because they already passed a similarly rigorous exam through Novell, Banyan, Sun, or Microsoft. These professionals are already skilled and possess certificates to prove it. Microsoft grants them MCSE certificates after they pass only five additional Microsoft exams.

Specifically, Microsoft automatically grants credit for the Networking Essentials exam once you've passed a Microsoft Certified Professional (MCP) exam and provide evidence that you hold one of these exact certificates:

1. Novell

   CNE—Certified Novell Engineer

   CNI—Certified Novell Instructor

   ECNE—Enterprise Certified Novell Engineer

   MCNE—Master Certified Novell Engineer

2. Banyan

   CBE—Certified Banyan CBE

   CBS—Certified Banyan Specialist

3. Sun

   CNA—Sun Certified Network Administrators for Solaris 2.5

   CNA—Sun Certified Network Administrators for Solaris 2.6

In addition to the networking certificates from Banyan, Novell, and Sun that can substitute for passing the Networking Essentials exam, there are two more ways to achieve an MCSE with only five (additional) exams. If you happen to have taken and passed one of the following two retired Microsoft exams, you can use that previous exam to have the Networking Essentials exam MCSE requirement waived.

Exam 70-046: Networking with Microsoft Windows for Workgroups 3.11 (retired)

Or

Exam 70-047: Networking with Microsoft Windows 3.1 (retired)

Retired Microsoft exams are explained in detail later in this chapter.

So, if you already hold one of the previously described certificates, or, if you have taken and passed one of the two retired Microsoft exams just listed, just pass one MCP exam and provide proof of your previous networking certificate, and you'll receive credit for two exams for the price of one.

WHAT IS AN MCP EXAM?

An MCP exam is a Microsoft exam. Passing an MCP exam makes you a Microsoft Certified Professional and automatically enrolls you in the Microsoft MCP program. But not all Microsoft exams are MCP exams. Networking Essentials, for instance, is not an MCP exam. The sidebar has more information about the MCP designation.

MICROSOFT CERTIFIED PROFESSIONALS (MCP)

Microsoft Certified Professionals [Microsoft Certified Professional] get their certificates by passing a Microsoft exam based on a Windows server or desktop operating system. NOTE: Not all MCP exams contribute to an MCSE certificate. In fact, not very many do. Be sure to check the official Microsoft requirements when you make your MCSE plans, to assure yourself that requirements have not changed since this study guide was written. Here are all the MCP exams that, as of this writing, can contribute toward an MCSE certification:

MCP Exams in the Windows NT 4.0 MCSE Track

70-030: Microsoft Windows 3.1 (retires September 1998)

70-048: Microsoft Windows for Workgroups 3.11—Desktop (retires September 1998)

70-064: Implementing and Supporting Microsoft Windows 95

70-067: Implementing and Supporting Microsoft Windows NT Server 4.0

70-073: Implementing and Supporting Microsoft Windows NT Workstation 4.0

MCP Exams in the Windows NT 3.51 MCSE Track

70-030: Microsoft Windows 3.1 (retires September 1998)

70-042: Implementing and Supporting Windows NT Workstation
3.51 (retires when Windows NT Workstation 5.0 exam is released)

70-043: Implementing and Supporting Windows NT Server 3.51
(retires when Windows NT Server 5.0 exam is released)

70-048: Microsoft Windows for Workgroups 3.11—Desktop (retires
September 1998)

70-064: Implementing and Supporting Microsoft Windows 95

Every MCSE certificate holder has multiple MCP designations
because of the nature of the MCSE requirements.

There is also a "premium" MCP certificate called *MCP+Internet*
available. MCP certificates are considered the basic Microsoft certificate leading to a premium MCP certificate or, in many cases, to
MCSE status. MCPs have a private Microsoft Web site, a free maga-
zine, other benefits, and a special logo of their own. Here is the URL
for the Microsoft MCP Web site:

Microsoft Certified Professional Web site—Certification Home Page
http://www.microsoft.com/mcp

By taking an MCP exam early in the MCSE process, you can gain
access to the MCP benefits just mentioned, which are valuable to
obtaining an MCSE as well.

MCSE Myth 2—Only One Year to Finish
Reality—Take As Long As You Want to Finish Your MCSE

Take as much time as you need to be prepared for each test. There
is no stated time limit for completion of the MCSE certificate.
Take examinations when you are ready. Although there is a popular misconception that you have only one year (or two years or
whatever) to complete your MCSE certificate, there is, in fact, no
time limit. The only limits are your own motivation and the time
available in your life. As an adult, you can decide for yourself how
much more of your life you want to spend working as something
other than an MCSE.

So, you should plan to progress at your own deliberate or expe-
ditious speed, depending on your needs, your personal learning
style, and the amount of time, money, and concentration you can
devote to this project. Everyone starts their MCSE studies with
different personal backgrounds, different circumstances, and different knowledge. Each reader brings different expectations for
this book. Some readers will want a guide:

- To confirm they already know enough to be certified
- To accompany a class or even a crash course
- To study on their own, reading and applying the concepts as they go

Not having an MCSE time limit is also consistent with good educational design, because adults learn best at their own rates, and in their own ways. It also keeps Microsoft away from the "bad guy" enforcer role. This way Microsoft never has to say, *"Sorry, all your work was for nothing, you're too late—you must start over."*

WHAT IF IT TAKES TOO LONG?
There is a possible downside to extending your MCSE studies. The longer you take, the more likely it is that one of the exams you've already passed will be retired *before* you finish your MCSE studies. If an exam you've passed is retired while you are still pursuing your MCSE, you'll need to replace the retired exam with a current exam, causing you more work to accomplish the same original goal.

Another reason to progress toward your MCSE with all due dispatch is in recognition of your own personal learning style. Many adults learn best if they concentrate heavily on learning, passing exams as a kind of punctuation in their study cycles. Also, each exam has areas of overlap with other exams. What you learn for one exam will help with other exams. Taking exam B soon after taking exam A, while the learning for exam A is still fresh in your memory, can be ideal for some adult learners. Adjust your exam strategy to accommodate your own learning style.

Establish a timeline for yourself. The longer you take to complete the MCSE track, the less likely you are to finish. Establish a study and examination schedule for yourself and make a serious effort to stick to the schedule and complete the exams in a timely manner. People generally work better if the end is in sight, so help yourself by creating a game plan for your certification.

MCSE Myth 3—Two-Week Wait for a Retest
Reality—First Retest Anytime, Second Retest After Two Weeks

Although there have been several changes instituted to improve security around the MCSE exams, as of now it is still okay to retake a failed exam as soon as you want. So, you can reschedule the same exam and retest as soon as you please—at full price, of course, if it happens that

- You fell asleep during the exam.
- You just had a bad day and only missed passing by one question.
- You were coming down with the flu the day of the exam.
- You otherwise failed an exam in a fluke event that did not represent your true level of mastery of the material.

If you fail twice, however, you will be required to wait at least two weeks before trying a third time.

> **TIP**
> Many MCSE candidates, and MCSE certificate holders, are convinced that certain questions appear on more than one exam. It seems to others that one or two questions are pulled from their "mother" exam and placed at random on other exams, without a discernable pattern. They claim that questions they expected on the TCP/IP exam turned up on the Windows NT Server or the Enterprise exam, for instance. Building a strong personal foundation of knowledge and experience is the only defense against this sort of random substitution, if it occurs.
>
> It is clear that the exams are at least quasi hierarchical, in that almost all Windows NT Workstation questions are legitimate fodder for the Windows NT Server exam, and all Windows NT Server exam questions are fair game for the Windows NT Server in the Enterprise exam, for instance. Likewise, all Networking Essentials questions are also fair game on the TCP/IP exam. This is another reason to take the exams in a deliberate, thoughtful order that makes sense with your own experience and knowledge.

MCSE Myth 4—You Must Pass Exam A *Before* Exam B
Reality—There Is No Required Exam Sequence

WHICH EXAM SHOULD YOU TAKE FIRST?

Please understand that there is no required sequence at all. You can literally take the MCSE exams in any order you please and achieve your certificate with no prejudice based on the order of your exams. However, there are good reasons why you might want to consider a purposeful rather than a random sequence of tests.

Here is a sample way to plan your studies. It's based on four assumptions, which may or may not be true for you:

1. You aren't already certifiable in one or more exam areas.

2. You don't have more extensive experience and knowledge in some exam areas than the others.

3. You've decided to take the following four exams, for example, to satisfy the core requirements for the MCSE:

   70-058: Networking Essentials

   70-067: Implementing and Supporting Microsoft Windows NT Server 4.0

   70-068: Implementing and Supporting Microsoft Windows NT Server 4.0 in the Enterprise

   70-073: Implementing and Supporting Microsoft Windows NT Workstation 4.0

4. You've decided to take the following two exams, for example, to satisfy the elective requirements for the MCSE:

   70-059: Internetworking with Microsoft TCP/IP on Windows NT 4.0

   70-077: Implementing and Supporting Microsoft Internet Information Server 3.0 and Microsoft Index Server 1.1

If these exams and givens fit your case, you might want to proceed in one of the following suggested exam sequences. First, check out the sidebar for basic suggestions for sequencing all MCSE exams.

SUGGESTIONS FOR MCSE EXAM SEQUENCING

Take the exam(s) you are *already* better prepared for first, if possible, to get things rolling and to begin your benefits as an MCP. Current Microsoft MCP benefits are summarized in another sidebar.

Take the more fundamental exam first, if one exam is a building block for another exam. This allows you to begin laying the conceptual and learning foundation for more complex ideas.

Take exams that have fair-to-high overlaps in Table 1-1 one after the other, if possible.

Take exams that will be easiest for you either at the beginning or at the end of the sequence, or as a deliberate break between tougher exams that are more challenging to you.

Table 1-1. Some Exams Overlap More Than Others. The Windows NT Server and the Windows NT Server in the Enterprise Exams Have a High Degree of Overlap.

Perceived Exam Overlaps	Networking Essentials	Windows NT Work-station	Windows NT Server	NT Server in the Enterprise	TCP/IP
Networking Essentials					
NT Work-station	low				
NT Server	low	high			
NT Server/ Enterprise	fair	low	high		
TCP/IP	high	low	low	low	
IIS and Index Server	low	low	fair	fair	high
Windows 95	low	low	low	low	fair
Exchange Server 5.0	low	low	fair	fair	fair

ENTERPRISE, SERVER, WORKSTATION

Table 1-1 estimates the overlap of content and knowledge areas between several popular exams. Of these, the three most closely related exams are the Windows NT Workstation, the Windows NT Server, and the Windows NT Server in the Enterprise exams. It makes sense to take these three exams in that order (Workstation, Server, and Enterprise), unless you already have extensive or special expertise in Windows NT Server or Windows NT Server in the Enterprise.

Of the exams listed in Table 1-1, the four generally considered to be the toughest are Windows NT Server in the Enterprise, TCP/IP on Microsoft Windows NT (any version), Windows 95 (retired), and Exchange Server 5.0. As usual, the exam that will be the toughest for you is the exam for which you are unprepared.

TCP/IP, NETWORKING ESSENTIALS, IIS AND INDEX SERVER

The next strongest relationship among the exams is the high degree of overlap between TCP/IP and both the Networking Essentials exam and the IIS and Index Server exam. Because Networking Essentials is considered the foundation of standards and definitions needed for networking concepts used in other exams, Networking Essentials is often taken early in the exam sequence.

As said, TCP/IP is judged to be one of the more difficult exams, even after the exam was redesigned to moderate the impact of subnetting.

And IIS and Index Server is commonly considered one of the most straightforward MCSE exams, largely because MCSE candidates are familiar with how to prepare for Microsoft exams by the time they attempt IIS and Index Server. IIS and Index Server also covers a more limited amount of material than the other exams, making it a quicker study.

So, combining all these information sources, here are some acceptable proposed exam sequences:

Exam Sequence A

1. Networking Essentials
2. Workstation
3. Server
4. Enterprise
5. TCP/IP
6. IIS and Index Server

Exam Sequence B

1. Networking Essentials
2. TCP/IP
3. Workstation
4. Server
5. IIS and Index Server
6. Enterprise

Exam Sequence C

1. Workstation

2. Networking Essentials

3. Server

4. Enterprise

5. TCP/IP

6. IIS and Index Server

If you selected other exams for your MCSE, rather than the six used in these examples, use these same principles to find your own ideal exam sequence.

SOME NETWORKING EXPERTS FIND MICROSOFT EXAMS DIFFICULT

It is not uncommon for networking professionals, with years of actual experience, to fail the **Networking Essentials** exam. Likewise, it is often heard that the **TCP/IP** exam is considered tough by seasoned Internet experts. Why is this so?

The most satisfying explanation is that these professionals already *know too much* about real-world networking, and they "read into" the exams real-world facts that are not stated in the question. Many Microsoft exam questions are stated ambiguously, and the resultant vagueness seems to force these professionals to make assumptions. They assume that if the question says *X*, and they know that *X* is almost always because of *Y*, then *Z* must be true—only to find that *Z* is not even an available answer!

Network professionals advise that, for their colleagues taking the Networking Essentials or TCP/IP exams from Microsoft, nothing from the real world should be assumed. Read the questions at face value only, to avoid reading anything real into the question. Often the questions that are the most troubling to these experts are simply testing their factual knowledge, rather than their troubleshooting expertise and network design experience.

Therefore, networking professionals with extensive prior experience often hold these two exams (Networking Essentials and TCP/IP) to the end of their exam sequence, hoping to get into the flow of the Microsoft testing manner of thinking before encountering these too-familiar topics.

BETA EXAMS ARE HALF PRICE

When a new exam is under construction, Microsoft "tests" the exam questions on folks like you and me. For $50, rather than the regular, full price of $100, we can take, and possibly pass, an exam while it is still in its "beta" stage.

You should expect beta exams to have between 150 and 200 questions, because they contain all the questions being considered for all versions of that exam. On a beta exam, you'll have *only* three hours to answer all the questions. This means that on a beta exam you must work at least at the same rapid pace you would use on a regular exam, if not faster.

Although beta exams can save you some money, they can also be frustrating, because it takes six to eight weeks to get your scores back from Microsoft. Waiting that long can be quite traumatic when you're used to having immediate results as you leave the testing room!

NOTE: Beta exams are designated with a *71* at the beginning of the exam code number, rather than the regular exam codes that begin with a *70*.

To find out if any beta exams are available, check this URL:

MCP Exam Information

http://www.microsoft.com/mcp/examinfo/exams.htm

Another point should be made about the Web page just cited. The dynamic links on the page jump to the official Microsoft Preparation Guides for each upcoming examination. Notice that the preparation guides become available *even before* the beta exams. This means you can actually be studying for an exam at the same time that it's being prepared to test your skills.

However, to study before the beta exam exists will sometimes require you to have access to the beta software product that the exam is based on. One of the many benefits of obtaining an MCSE certificate is a one-year subscription to the Microsoft Beta Evaluation program—free monthly CDs containing Microsoft beta software.

As of April 1998, these exams were *expected soon* in beta form:

Beta exam expected **July 1998**

Beta exam 71-098: Implementing and Supporting Microsoft **Windows 98** for
Exam 70-098: Implementing and Supporting Microsoft **Windows 98**

Preparation Guide for exam 70-098 at: http://www.microsoft.com/mcp/exam/stat/SP70-098.htm

Beta exam expected **summer 1998**
> *Beta exam 71-028:* System Administration for Microsoft **SQL Server** 7.0 for
> Exam 70-028: System Administration for Microsoft **SQL Server** 7.0

Preparation Guide for exam 70-028 at
> http://www.microsoft.com/mcp/exam/stat/SP70-028.htm

Beta exam expected **summer 1998**
> Beta exam 71-055: Developing Solutions with Microsoft **Front-Page 98** for
> Exam 70-055: Developing Solutions with Microsoft **FrontPage 98**

Preparation Guide for exam 70-055 at:
> http://www.microsoft.com/mcp/exam/stat/SP70-055.htm

Beta exam expected **fall 1998**
> *Beta exam 71-086:* Implementing and Supporting Microsoft **Systems Management Server** 2.0 for
> Exam 70-086: Implementing and Supporting Microsoft **Systems Management Server** 2.0

Preparation Guide for Exam 70-086 at:
> http://www.microsoft.com/mcp/exam/stat/SP70-086.htm

Beta exam expected **fall 1998**
> *Beta exam 71-029:* Implementing a Database Design on Microsoft **SQL Server** 7.0 for
> Exam 70-029: Implementing a Database Design on Microsoft **SQL Server** 7.0

Preparation Guide for exam 70-029 at:
> http://www.microsoft.com/mcp/exam/stat/SP70-029.htm

Old Exams Are Eventually Retired

Yes, Microsoft retires old exams. However, they take several specific measures to mollify the effect of obsolete exams on certified professionals—including giving six months advance warning in writing and substantially cutting the cost of replacement exams for at least six months *after* the former exam is retired. Read on for the details.

When an operating system (OS) is no longer commonly in use, supporting the old operating system becomes increasingly expensive. If new and better operating systems are available at reasonable prices, and the migration path for the majority of users is not too burdensome, it stands to reason that the manufacturer would want to withdraw the old OS from support. Similarly, Microsoft examinations are withdrawn and retired when their use has waned, especially when the OS they are based on is becoming obsolete.

In explaining Microsoft's policy on retirement of exams, it's useful to know that they highly value the relevance of the *skills measured by the exams.* If your skills are still in demand in the marketplace, there will be less reason to retire the exam that certified those skills. Microsoft explains that their exam retirement decisions are based on several factors, including:

- Total number of copies of the product ever sold (the customer base)
- Total number of exams ever taken (the MCP base)
- Ongoing sales of corresponding Microsoft products
- Ongoing sales of corresponding Microsoft courseware

By considering this broad framework, Microsoft can retire only exams that have fallen out of use and have truly become obsolete.

Microsoft announces which exams are being withdrawn and retired, at this URL:

Microsoft Certified Professional Web site—Retired MCP Exams Information
http://www.microsoft.com/mcp/examinfo/retired.htm

If your MCSE certificate is based on an exam that is being, or has been, retired, you'll probably need to find a replacement exam to prepare for and pass, to position your certificate for renewal.

What Happens When One of My Exams Is Retired?

Although there are no guarantees that these policies will always be the same, here are the current Microsoft policies on exam retirements. First, you'll be mailed a notification in writing at least six months *before* your certification is affected. Then, you'll be given a date deadline to pass specific replacement exam(s). You may take all replacement exams at a 50 percent discount until at least six months after the exam retirement date. For any questions or comments about Microsoft exam retirements, or if you ever want to check your certification status or ask about the MCSE program in general, just send e-mail to mcp@msprograms.com or call one of the following Microsoft regional education centers:

North America:	800-636-7544
Asia and Pacific:	61-2-9870-2250
Europe:	353-1-7038774
Latin America:	801-579-2829

In addition, there are many more toll-free numbers for Microsoft International Training & Certification Customer Service Centers in several dozen countries worldwide at this URL:

Microsoft Training & Certification Programs—International Training and Certification Customer Service Centers http://www.microsoft.com/train_cert/resc.htm

One more thought on retiring exams: Because an MCSE certificate is good for life, or until exams are retired, the *only way* to be sure that MCSE professionals are keeping up with the real-world information-technology market is for Microsoft to retire exams. For the MCSE to continue to signify the highest level of professional skills, old exams must be retired and replaced with more current exams based on skills currently in demand.

EARLY WARNING OF EXAM RETIREMENT
One of the earliest warnings that an exam you've taken may become obsolete is that the development of a new exam is announced for the next version of the software, or a beta exam is announced for a new version of the exam. Once beta software or a beta exam has appeared, watch for further signs more closely.

Usually, there is advance warning that an exam is being withdrawn many months before the event. If you subscribe to the following monthly mailing lists and read the Web pages mentioned, you'll have the longest forewarning to choose how you'll prepare for any changes.

MCP News Flash (monthly)—includes exam announcements and special promotions

Training and Certification News (monthly)—about training and certification at Microsoft

To subscribe to either newsletter, visit this Web page, register with Microsoft, and then subscribe:

Personal Information Center
    http://207.46.130.169/regwiz/forms/PICWhyRegister.htm

Don't be caught off guard. Stay in touch with the status of the MCSE exams you've invested in mastering!

Free Sample Exam Software CD-ROM

Microsoft will ship (by UPS—United Parcel Service—so that an ordinary United States Postal Service post office box address won't work) a CD containing a dated snapshot of the Microsoft Certified Professional (MCP) Web site and sample examination software called Personal Exam Prep (PEP) exams.

By calling Microsoft in the United States or Canada at (800) 636-7544, you can request the most recent CD of the MCP Web site. Ask for the "Roadmap CD." They may protest greatly—don't worry. They'll say the "Roadmap to Certification CD" is no longer available, and that you would be much better off to check the Microsoft Web site for more up-to-date information. However, they'll also still (as of this writing) ship a CD if you insist, and if you provide an address *other than a post office box.*

Of course, if you're in a hurry, you can always download the free sample exam software directly from the Microsoft Web site at:

Personal Exam Prep (PEP) Tests
    http://www.microsoft.com/mcp/examinfo/practice.htm
    (mspep.exe) (561K)

The free PEP exam download currently covers these Microsoft tests:

70-018: Implementing and Supporting Microsoft Systems Management Server 1.2

70-026: System Administration of Microsoft SQL Server 6

70-058: Networking Essentials

70-059: Internetworking with Microsoft TCP/IP on Windows NT 4.0

70-063: Implementing and Supporting Microsoft Windows 95 (retired)

70-067: Implementing and Supporting Microsoft Windows NT Server 4.0

70-068: Implementing and Supporting Microsoft Windows NT Server 4.0 in the Enterprise

70-073: Implementing and Supporting Microsoft Windows NT Workstation 4.0

70-075: Implementing and Supporting Microsoft Exchange Server 4.0

70-077: Implementing and Supporting Microsoft Internet Information Server 3.0 and Microsoft Index Server 1.1

70-160: Microsoft Windows Architecture I

70-165: Developing Application with Microsoft Visual Basic 5.0

Free Personal Exam Prep (PEP) Test Software

The PEP sample exam software has many values. First, you should take the appropriate PEP exam as the *beginning* of your studies for each new exam. This mere act commits you to the course of study for that exam and offers you a valid taste of the depth and breadth of the real exam. Seeing what kind of material is on the exams also allows you to recognize the actual level of detail expected on the exams, so that you can avoid studying too much or too little to pass the exam.

Later, by taking the PEP examination again from time to time, you can generally gauge your progress through the material. The PEP exam also gives you practice at taking an exam on a computer. Perhaps best of all, it allows you to print the questions and answers for items you may have missed, so that you can concentrate on areas where your understanding is weakest.

Although the PEP tests are written by Self Test Software, they are distributed free by Microsoft to assist MCP candidates in preparing for the real exams. Take advantage of this generous offer!

Several other sources of practice exam software, including several more free samples, are provided in a sidebar later in this chapter.

Prepare for Each Exam

Free TechNet CD

The value of this offer cannot be overestimated. The free TechNet Trial CD includes the entire Microsoft knowledge base, plus many evaluation and deployment guides, white papers, and all the text from the Microsoft resource kits. This information is straight from the horse's mouth and is therefore indispensable to your successful studies for the MCSE certificate. And the price can't be beat. Do not delay, get this free TechNet CD today!

Of course, Microsoft is hoping you'll actually subscribe to TechNet. Once you have earned the MCSE certificate, you probably will be sure to convince your employer to subscribe, if you don't subscribe yourself. TechNet can help you solve obscure problems more quickly; it can help you keep up-to-date with fast-paced technology developments inside and outside of Microsoft; and it can help you keep your bosses and your users happy.

Microsoft TechNet ITHome—Get a Free TechNet Trial Subscription
http://204.118.129.122/giftsub/Clt1Form.asp

On the same Web page you can also register for ITHome and other free newsletters.

Remember, Microsoft exams generally don't require you to recall obscure information. Common networking situations and ordinary administrative tasks are the real focus. Exam topics include common circumstances, ordinary issues, and popular network problems that networking and operating system experts are confronted with every day.

Use Practice Exams

Taking a practice exam early helps you focus your study on the topics and level of detail appropriate for the exam. As already mentioned, taking another practice exam later can help you gauge how well your studies are progressing. Many professionals wait until their practice exams' scores are well above the required passing score for that exam, then they take the real exam.

There are many sources of practice exams, and most of the vendors offer free samples of some kind. Microsoft supplies free sample exams from Self Test Software, and the MCSE mailing lists on the Internet often recommend products from Transcender. Both of these and several other practice exam sources are listed in the sidebar.

PRACTICE EXAMS AVAILABLE—FREE SAMPLES

BeachFrontQuizzer
E-mail: info@bfq.com
http://www.bfq.com/
Phone: 888/992-3131

A free practice exam (for Windows NT 4.0 Workstation) is available for download.

LearnKey
http://www.learnkey.com/
Phone: 800/865-0165
Fax: 435/674-9734
1845 W. Sunset Blvd.
St. George, UT 84770-6508

MasterExam simulation software—$800 for six exam simulations, or $150 each.

NetG
info@netg.com
support@netg.com
http://www.netg.com/
800/265-1900 (in United States only)
630/369-3000
Fax: 630/983-4518

NETg International
info@uk.netg.com
1 Hogarth Business Park
Burlington Lane
Chiswick, London
England W4 2TJ
Phone: 0181-994-4404
Fax: 0181-994-5611

Supporting Microsoft Windows NT 4.0 Core Technologies—Part 1 (course 71410 - Unit 1 - 7.7 MB) and Microsoft FrontPage Fundamentals (course 71101 - Unit 2 - 8.1 MB) are available as free sample downloads.

Prep Technologies, Inc.
Sales@mcpprep.com
Support@mcpprep.com
http://www.mcpprep.com/
1-888/627-7737 (1-888/MCP-PREP)
1-708/478-8684 (outside US)

CICPreP (Computer Industry Certification Preparation from ITS, Inc.)
A free 135-question practice exam is available for download (5+ MB).

Self Test Software
feedback@stsware.com
http://www.stsware.com/
Americas
Toll-Free: 1-800/244-7330 (Canada and USA)
Elsewhere: 1-770/641-1489
Fax 1-770/641-9719

Self Test Software Inc.
4651 Woodstock Road
Suite 203, M/S 384
Roswell, GA 30075-1686

Australia/Asia
E-mail address stsau@vue.com
Phone: 61-2-9320-5497
Fax: 61-2-9323-5590
Sydney, Australia

Europe/Africa
The Netherlands
Phone: 31-348-484646
Fax: 31-348-484699

$79 for the first practice exam, $69 for additional practice exams ordered at the same time.
Twelve free practice exams are available for download. These are the same free practice exams that Microsoft distributes by download or CD.

Transcender
Product Questions: sales@transcender.com
Technical Support Questions: support@transcender.com
Demo Download Problems: troubleshooting@transcender.com
http://www.transcender.com/

Phone: 615/726-8779
Fax: 615/726-8884
621 Mainstream Drive, Suite 270
Nashville, TN 37228-1229

Fifteen free practice exams are available for download.

VFX Technologies, Inc
sales@vfxtech.com
support@vfxtech.com
http://www.vfxtech.com/
Phone: 610/265.9222
Fax: 610/265.6007
POB 80222
Valley Forge, PA 19484-0222 USA

Twenty-two free practice MCP Endeavor exam preparation modules
are available for download.

Organize Before Day of Exam

Make sure you have plenty of time to study before each exam.
You know yourself. Give yourself enough time to both study *and*
get plenty of sleep for at least two days before the exam. Make
sure coworkers, family, and friends are aware of the importance of
this effort, so that they will give you the time and space to devote
to your studies.

Once you have the materials and equipment you need, and
study times and locations properly selected—force yourself to
study and practice. Reward yourself when you finish a segment or
unit of studying. Pace yourself so that you complete your study
plan on time.

Survey Testing Centers

Call each testing center in your area to find out what times they
offer Microsoft exams. Jot down the center's name, address, and
phone number, along with the testing hours and days of the
week. Once you've checked the testing hours at all the centers in
your local area, you're in a better position to schedule an exam at
center B if center A is already booked for the time you wanted to
take your next exam.

The Sylvan technician taking your registration may not easily
find all other testing centers near you, so be prepared to suggest

alternative testing center names for the technician to locate, in the event that your first choice is not available.

Plan to take your MCSE exams at a time of your own choice, after you know when exams are available in your area. This puts you in control and allows you to take into account your own life situation and your own style. If you are sharpest in the early morning, take the exams in the morning. If you can't get calm enough for an exam until late afternoon, schedule your exams for whatever time of day, or phase of the moon, that best suits you. If you really need to have a special time slot, schedule your exam well in advance.

Same-Day and Weekend Testing

You may be able to schedule an exam on the same day that you call to register, if you're lucky. This special service requires the test vendor, Sylvan or VUE, to download the exam to or store the exam at the testing site especially for you, and it requires the testing site to have an open slot at a time acceptable to your needs. Sometimes this works out, and sometimes it doesn't. Most testing centers are interested in filling all available exam time slots, so if you get a wild hair to take an exam *today,* why not give it a try? VUE (Virtual University Enterprises, a division of National Computer Systems, Inc.) testing centers can schedule exams for you, and they store exams on-site, so they are especially well positioned for same-day testing.

Shop Around for Best Testing Center Available

Shop around your area for the best testing center. Some testing centers are distractingly busy and noisy at all times. Some official testing centers have slow 25-MHz computers, small 12-inch monitors, cramped seating conditions, or distracting activity outside the windows. Some centers occasionally even have crabby, uninformed staff. Other centers actually limit testing to certain hours or certain days of the week, rather than allowing testing during all open hours.

These MCSE exams are important to your career—you deserve to use the best testing environment available. The best center costs the same $100 that a less-pleasant center does. Shop around and find out exactly what is available in your area.

If you are treated improperly, or if appropriate services or accommodations were not available when they should have been, let Sylvan or VUE, and Microsoft, know by e-mail and telephone.

Check for Aviation Testing Centers

Some of the best testing centers are actually at airports. Aviation training centers, located at all major airports to accommodate pilots, are frequently well equipped and pleasant environments. Aviation training centers participate in Microsoft testing to better use their investment in computer testing rooms, and to broaden their customer base.

The best thing about aviation training centers is that they are regularly open all day on weekends, both Saturday and Sunday. The staff at some aviation training centers actually like to work on weekends. One verified example, for instance, of an aviation training center and excellent Microsoft testing center available all day every weekend is Wright Flyers in San Antonio, Texas, telephone: 210/820-3800 or e-mail: Wflyers@Flash.Net.

Official Exam Registration and Scheduling

VUE exam scheduling and rescheduling services are available on weekends and evenings; in fact, they're open on the World Wide Web 24 hours a day, 365 days a year. Sylvan's telephone hours are Monday through Friday, 7:00 A.M. through 7:00 P.M., central time, and the new Saturday telephone hours are 7:00 A.M. through 3:00 P.M.

As mentioned, many testing centers are open weekends on both Saturday and Sunday. If something goes horribly wrong at a Sylvan testing center after 3:00 P.M. on Saturday, or anytime on Sunday, you'll have to wait to talk to Sylvan when they open on Monday morning. As has happened, if a testing center simply fails to open its doors for your scheduled exam while Sylvan is closed for the weekend, you can do nothing until Monday morning.

Install Software and Try Each Option

Make sure you know the layout of the various options in the software's graphical user interface (GUI), and which popular configuration options are set on each menu. Become "GUI familiar" with each software product required in your next exam by opening and studying each and every option on each and every menu. Also, for whatever they're worth, read the Help files, especially any context-sensitive Help.

Commonly tested everyday network features, like controlling access to sensitive resources, printing over the network, client and server software installation, configuration, troubleshooting, load balancing, fault tolerance, and combinations of these topics (such as security-sensitive printing over the network) are especially important. Remember, the exams are from the network administrator's point of view. Imagine what issues network designers, technical support specialists, and network administrators are faced with every day—those are the issues that will be hit hardest on the exams.

MCSE candidates are expected to be proficient at planning, renovating, and operating Microsoft networks that are well integrated with Novell networks, with IBM LANs and IBM mainframes, with network printers (with their own network interface cards), and with other common network services. Microsoft expects you to be able to keep older products, especially older Microsoft products, running as long as possible, and to know when they finally must be upgraded, and how to accomplish the upgrade or migration with the least pain and expense.

Pass One Exam at a Time

Microsoft exams are experience-based and require real know-how, not just book learning. Don't be fooled by anyone—you must have real experience with the hardware and software involved to excel on the exams, or as an MCSE holder in the workplace.

Passing a Microsoft exam is mostly a statement that you have the experience and knowledge that are required. And there is also an element in passing of knowing how to deal with the exam situation, one question at a time. This section describes the various kinds of questions you'll encounter on the MCSE exams and gives you pointers and tips about successful strategies for dealing with each kind of question.

This section then walks you through the process of scheduling an exam, arriving at the test center, and taking the exam. There is also a brief resource list of additional sources of information related to topics in this chapter.

Kinds of MCSE Exam Questions
Choose the Best Answer

These questions are the most popular, because they are seemingly simple questions. "Choose the best answer" means *one* answer, but the fact that there is only one answer doesn't make the question easy—unless you know the material.

First, try to eliminate at least two obviously wrong answers. This narrows the field, so that you can choose among the remaining options more easily.

SOME QUESTIONS INCLUDE EXHIBITS

Briefly look at the exhibit when you *begin* to read the question. Note important features in the exhibit, then finish a careful reading of the whole question. Return to the exhibit after you've read the entire question to check on any relevant details revealed in the question.

Some exhibits have nothing to do with answering the question correctly, so don't waste your time on the exhibit if it has no useful information for finding the solution.

Choose All That Apply

The most obviously tough questions are those with an uncertain number of multiple choices: "Choose all that apply." Here, you should use the same procedure to eliminate wrong answers first. Select only the items that you have confidence in—don't be tempted to take a wild guess. Remember, the Microsoft exams do not allow partial credit for partial answers, so any wrong answer is deadly, even if you got the rest of the question right!

Really Read Scenario Questions

There is no better advice for these killer questions. Read the scenario questions carefully and completely. These seemingly complex questions are composed of several parts, generally in this pattern:

1. A few short paragraphs describing the situation, hardware, software, and the organization involved, possibly including one or two exhibits that must be opened, studied, and then minimized or closed again

2. The required results

3. Two or three optional desired results

4. The proposed solution

5. Four multiple choice answers you must choose among

Most scenario questions have an opening screen that warns that you should "Pay close attention to the number of optional results specified in answer B." This instruction is to accommodate the fact that there are sometimes two, and sometimes three, optional results, and to accommodate occasional proposed solutions that only satisfy the required result and some (but not all) of the optional results.

Often two scenario questions in a row will differ only in their proposed solutions. They'll have the same scenario, the same exhibit, the same results, but different solutions will be proposed. Sometimes some other slight difference might be introduced in the second scenario. Compare those similar questions, noting the differences to see what's missing, or what's new, in the second question. If the second question satisfies all the required and desired results, that tends to imply that the *previous* scenario did not satisfy all optional results, at least.

Also, it is common to encounter another scenario question later in the same exam, which clarifies the situation in the previous scenario. Some people jot down the question numbers and topics of each scenario, to enable them to return and reconsider a question after reading other, related questions and perhaps having a flash of memory that might help.

TIP
The scuttlebutt is that, if you just don't have a clue on a complex scenario question, or if you're out of time, you should select answer A (meets all results) or D (meets none), because these are the most frequently correct answers. The recommended method, of course, is to know the material better, so that you never need to resort to this kind of superstitious advantage.

For most people, your first priority should be to note the required results. If the proposed solution does not satisfy the required result, you're done with the question and you can move on. There is no need to focus on the optional desired results unless the required result is satisfied.

There can be up to three optional desired results, and each one must be evaluated independently. Usually, if an optional result is satisfied, there are specific words in the question that deal with the optional result. Use the practice exams to sharpen your skills at quickly identifying which optional results are satisfied by which words in the question.

Another strategy that works for some people is to focus first on the question and results (both required and optional), writing down all related facts based on the question's wording. This strategy then evaluates the proposed solution, based on the previous question analysis. Because some people find the scenario questions to be ambiguously written and vague, this strategy can also lead to time wasted on unimportant or unnecessary analysis, especially if the proposed solution does not meet the required results.

Some people work at exams differently. Aside from intelligence, there are also very different learning and understanding styles among adults. Some people, for instance, find that they deal better with the scenario questions by working backward from the required results and, later, if necessary, from the optional results. They break the question into its elements, find their own solutions, and, then, finally compare notes with the solution proposed by the exam.

For example, they might start from the required results, building the case that would be required to create that final required result. Once they have built their own solutions that meet the required result, they then check their solutions against the exam's proposed solution. By checking their conclusions against the exam's proposed solution and the givens offered in the question, they then easily decide which required and optional results are achieved. If they know the material, they can answer the scenario questions; they just do it in a way others would call backward.

It's important for candidates to see the forest *and* the trees, and to know when to see each. In a question about a congested network, the candidate must decide whether the question is trying to ferret out the factual knowledge that FDDI (*Fiber Distributed Data Interface*) is faster than 802.3 10 Mbps Ethernet, or knowledge about the technical standards for, and installation and configuration details of, FDDI. Candidates with extensive networking experience may be tempted to show off and choose the latter, when only the simple knowledge that FDDI is faster than Ethernet was required. Don't read information into the question that is not there!

Exam Interface Quirks—Sylvan Interface

The Sylvan exam interface has a peculiar quirk on long questions that can hurt you if you're not careful. This is particularly true if the testing center uses small monitors, so that many questions are longer than one screen. On these long questions there is an elevator or scroll bar on the right side of the screen, so that you can use the mouse to move down to read the remainder of the question.

When you reach the bottom of the question, but not until you reach the bottom, the left selection box on the outside bottom of the screen changes from "More" to "Next." There is a built-in assumption that if you are not looking at the bottom of the screen when you select your answer, you've made a premature answer.

If you have moved back up the screen to reread the question, for example, and the very bottom of the screen is *not visible,* and you then check very near but not exactly on your answer, sometimes the box above your selection actually gets selected, rather than the box you intended to check. To correct for this quirk, either you should be sure you are always looking at the very bottom of the screen before you select the answer, or you should back up from the next question, by clicking on the "Previous" question box, to double-check your previous selection.

Select Wrong Answers

Okay, it sounds nuts. But the best advice around is to begin analysis of each question by selecting the answers that are clearly wrong. Every wrong answer eliminated gets you closer to the correct answer(s). Often there are two answers that can be quickly eliminated, leaving you to focus on fewer remaining options.

By carefully structuring your time, you can answer more questions correctly during the allotted exam period. Eliminate wrong and distracter answers first, to narrow your attention to the more likely correct answers.

Indirect Questions

Microsoft exams are not straightforward. They often use questions that *indirectly* test your skill and knowledge, without coming straight out and asking you about the facts they are testing. For example, there is no exam question that actually asks "Is the Windows NT 4.0 Emergency Repair Disk bootable?" and there is no question that says "The Windows NT 4.0 Emergency Repair Disk is not bootable, True or False?" But you had better know that the Emergency Repair Disk (ERD) is *never* bootable. By knowing that the ERD cannot be booted, you can eliminate at least one wrong answer and, therefore, come closer to the right answer on one or more exams. *By the way, after you've once had an unfortunate experience that calls for actually using the Windows NT ERD, you'll never again have a doubt about whether you can boot to it—the ERD repair occurs considerably later, well after booting the computer.*

After you've taken a Microsoft exam or two, if you think you would be good at composing their kind of indirect question that tests many facets and levels at the same time, check out this URL, where you can get information about being a contract test writer for Microsoft:

Microsoft Certified Professional Web site—Become a Contract
    Writer
`http://www.microsoft.com/Train_Cert/Mcp/examinfo/iwrite.htm`

Scheduling an Exam

Register by exam number. Say, "I want to register to take Microsoft exam number 70-058." Also know the exact title of the exam, so that it's familiar when the test registrar reads it back to you.

The Microsoft MCSE exams are administered by or through VUE (Virtual University Enterprises, a division of National Computer Systems, Inc.) or Sylvan Prometric. Either Sylvan or VUE can provide MCSE testing. Both VUE and Sylvan have access to your records of previous MCSE tests, and both vendors report your test results directly to Microsoft. Taking an examination through either vendor organization does not obligate you to use the same organization or the same testing center for any other examination.

VUE began testing for Microsoft in May 1998, after requests for another vendor from throughout the Microsoft professional community. They began by offering exams only in English and largely in North America. VUE projects significant growth during 1998 and 1999, with worldwide coverage available by June 1999.

Sylvan Prometric

To schedule yourself for an exam through Sylvan, or for information about the Sylvan testing center nearest you, call 800/755-3926 (800/755-exam) or write to Sylvan at:

Sylvan Prometric
Certification Registration
2601 88th Street West
Bloomington, MN 55431

To register online:

Sylvan Prometric (Nav1)
  http://www.slspro.com/

Sylvan also offers 16 short sample online exams, called *Assessment Tests*, on various Microsoft products. (*Although Sylvan has offered online registration for several months, reports have continued that would-be exam candidates are unable to use the online registration, despite valiant attempts—good luck!*)

Phone: 800/755-3926

Virtual University Enterprises (VUE)

To schedule yourself for an exam through VUE, or for information about the VUE testing center nearest you, call 888/837-8616 or visit VUE's Web site to register online 24 hours a day, 365 days a year:

Virtual University Enterprises (VUE)

To register online:

5001 W. 80th Street, Suite 401
Bloomington, MN 55437-1108
Phone: North America: 888/837-8616 toll-free
http://www.vue.com/ms

VUE is a new kid on the block; but never fear, they are seasoned test people, and their promise to the industry has been new thinking in technology and service, and higher levels of candidate and testing center service. They have a "we try harder" attitude and back it up with higher standards for testing centers (800 × 600 video resolution on Windows 95 machines) and an agile, new, 32-bit testing engine. While VUE is in expansion mode, you should expect some growing pains, but also watch for some new thinking and professional amiability.

For instance, VUE immediately found a way to offer live online 24-hour, seven-days-a-week exam scheduling and rescheduling of Microsoft exams for busy professionals. And VUE offers on-site exam scheduling and rescheduling at *testing centers*. These conveniences will be tremendously valuable to individual candidates. Because VUE's operation is based on heavy Internet bandwidth, they are able to use secure Java-based system management and site administration software to handle all testing and services. Also, VUE stores exams on-site and delivers new exams quickly to testing centers over the Internet, rather than by modem and telephone lines, as Sylvan does.

When You Arrive at the Testing Center

Arrive early. It can put you at ease to check in 30 to 60 minutes early. Relax a bit before you actually sit for the exam. Some exam centers won't complete your check-in until the last minute before your scheduled time, and others will get you all signed up and then tell you to "let them know" when you're ready to begin. Sometimes they'll offer to let you begin "early." Starting a little bit late is also sometimes tolerated, if you want to review your notes one more time—be sure to ask first.

To check in, you'll be asked to provide proof of your identity. Two pieces of ID with your name and signature are required, one must have a photograph of you—a driver's license or passport and a credit card are adequate. There are testing center rules you'll be asked to read, sign, and date. Microsoft has also begun to require, on all new exams, that the candidate agree to a nondisclosure statement, discussed in the next section.

Testing center staff will explain their procedures and show you to the testing computers. This is the time to ask any questions about the testing rules. Find out, for instance, if you'll be allowed to leave the exam room to visit the rest room (with the *clock still running* on your exam) if your physical comfort demands a break.

Carry Water Only

Some folks bring bottled water, vitamins, or medications into the exam room, for their own comfort. You should consider what will make you most productive during the 75 minutes of your exam, and prepare accordingly.

Of course, the downside to drinking soda, coffee, or water during or even before the exam occurs later, when you are nearing the end of the 90-minute exam and really need to visit the rest room instead of staying to finish.

Writing Material in the Exam Room

This is a touchy area. Testing centers are required to be very picky about *cheat notes* carried *into* or *out of* the exam. There is a story of a candidate who had an ordinary napkin wrapped around a can of soda in the exam room, and carried it out for disposal at the end of the exam. The candidate was challenged about the napkin, and would probably have been disqualified or worse had the napkin contained any writing.

Always ask for writing implements. Paper and pen are easier to use, but some testing centers will not allow them. Those centers that do not allow pen and paper will issue you marking pens and plasticized writing cards that are hard to use.

The marking pens commonly have a wide tip that makes writing difficult, and they dry out very quickly between uses if they will write at all—you must remember to replace the cap or the pen will fail to write the next time you try. Get the finest tipped pens available. The tips seem to widen with use, so newer pens are better. Ask the testing center to open a *new* package of pens, and ask for two or three pens in case they go completely dry.

Also ask for another sheet or two of the 8.5-by-10-inch plasticized writing material. If you have a large network drawing in mind, for instance, use the back of the card—2 inches of the card's front are already in use by Sylvan Prometric. Don't force yourself to try to use those awkward marking pens in a small space—start another side or another sheet!

TIP

Don't waste your precious exam time writing down any memorized notes on the exam room writing material. Write down any memorized notes during the time *before the exam* you could use for taking the how-to-use-this-exam-software tutorial (discussed next). Some exams call for more memorization than others, and some exams have a tremendous amount of minute detail. Use your time wisely by recording any easily forgotten formulae, rules of thumb, and mnemonics *before* you begin the exam, *after* you enter the exam room.

The day before the exam, practice writing down all those notes you've decided will help you on your exam. Force yourself to write from memory only, to prove you can remember them long enough to write them down in the exam room.

Online Tutorial

There is an optional exam tutorial available before each MCSE exam. The tutorial is designed to show you how the computer-administered exam software works and to help you become familiar with how the exam will proceed *before the clock starts on your real exam.* Don't become confused by the presence of the tutorial—if the clock in the upper-right corner is ticking, you are taking the real exam, not the tutorial!

NERVOUS?

If you happen to be nervous before an exam, it might help reduce your anxiety to take some off-the-clock time with the optional tutorial to breathe deeply and calm yourself down and get into the right mood for passing the exam. Even if you've already seen the tutorial and know exactly how to run the exam software, the tutorial can be a safety valve to give you a little time to adjust your attitude. Controlling your own use of time around the exam can give you just the boost you need.

Required Nondisclosure Agreement

Microsoft requires certification candidates to accept a nondisclosure agreement before taking some exams. If you take an exam that was first released after February 1998, you'll be required to provide an affirmation that you accept the terms of a brief, formal nondisclosure agreement. This policy will eventually cover all MCSE exams. Microsoft says this policy will help maintain the integrity of the MCP program. The text of the agreement is provided in the sidebar and is also available at this URL:

Microsoft Certified Professional Web site—Certification Nondisclosure Agreement for MCP Exams:

http://www.microsoft.com/mcp/articles/nda.htm

NONDISCLOSURE AGREEMENT AND GENERAL TERMS OF USE FOR EXAMS DEVELOPED FOR THE MICROSOFT CERTIFIED PROFESSIONAL PROGRAM

This exam is Microsoft confidential and is protected by trade secret law. It is made available to you, the examinee, solely for the purpose of becoming certified in the technical area referenced in the title of this exam. You are expressly prohibited from disclosing, publishing, reproducing, or transmitting this exam, in whole or in part, in any form or by any means, verbal or written, electronic or mechanical, for any purpose, without the prior express written permission of Microsoft Corporation.

Click the Yes button to symbolize your signature and to accept these terms. Click the No button if you do not accept these terms. You must click Yes to continue with the exam.

Mandatory Demographic Survey

Microsoft says they appreciate your participation in the mandatory demographic survey before each exam. For years the survey was optional—now it is mandatory. Microsoft estimates the survey will take most candidates less than five minutes. Of course, the survey time does not count against your clocked exam period.

To motivate you to furnish sincere and valid answers on the mandatory survey, Microsoft stresses that the survey results are vital to the program and useful for setting the passing score of each exam, for validating new exam questions, and in developing training materials for MCSE candidates. Microsoft says, "By providing accurate and complete information on this survey, you will help Microsoft improve both the quality of MCP exams and the value of your certification."

The mandatory demographic survey collects information, keyed to your Social Security number, about your work experience, your work environment, the software tested by the exam, and information about your exam preparation methods. The survey has three components. One portion is common to all exams, another is keyed to the exam track, and the third portion is specific to that one exam. Carefully note the wording of any promises of confidentiality, data cross matching, or disclosure of your personal information.

Check Exam Number and Exam Title

Although it is unlikely, there have been stories about the wrong test being loaded for an exam candidate. The first task when taking a Microsoft exam is to be sure you are beginning the exam *you intended to take*. By double-checking the exam number and exam title, you might save yourself and the testing center hours of difficulty, if somehow the wrong exam showed up for you. So, be sure you check the exam title before you begin the clock on the exam—checking the exam title doesn't need to be part of your timed exam.

Item Review Strategies

In the upper-right corner, there is a small square box with the word "Mark" next to it. This little box is your key to another method to better manage your time during MCSE exams. When you encounter a question that stumps you or leaves you feeling as though you didn't study the right material *at all,* check an answer with the best guess you can quickly make, check the "Mark" box, and move on to the next question. At the end of the exam there is an item review option that will allow you to revisit only the questions you marked. When you reach the end of the questions, a page that summarizes your answers to all the questions is shown. It has red marks where you have not yet completed the question or skipped it entirely. Try to fill in at least a best guess as you go through the exam the first time—you can't get a question right that was left blank or incomplete.

The end-of-exam summary page also shows which items you marked for later review. If you click on the box for Item Review, you will be taken back through your marked questions from the beginning of the exam, without needing to see the other, non-marked questions intervening. Or, if you double-click on any answer on the summary page, you'll be taken to that question, marked or not.

After you're quite comfortable with the testing process, you might want to consider this advanced strategy for dealing with marked questions. As you go through the exam, remember to jot down topics that are in the "stumper" questions you've marked. Then, if a later question includes that same topic, make a note of what the question number is, right next to your "tough topics" list. This way, when it comes time for you to review the questions you marked, you'll have the numbers of informative or "clue-filled" questions to review on that same topic. Although the final summary screen allows you to access any question, unless you've recorded the question number as you go along it may be too time consuming to find that informative question during item review.

Exam Room Notes

For the Networking Essentials exam, here are typical items to memorize and write down as soon as you enter the exam room, before the clock starts:

- Which IRQs are used by which services, and which IRQs are likely to be available?

- 10Base2, 10Base5, and 10BaseT maximum device nodes, cable and network trunk length maximums.

Sources of Additional Information

Microsoft maintains a large staff to handle your questions about the MCSE certificate. Give them a call at:

Microsoft MCP Program: 800/636-7544

If you have a CompuServe account, you can access the Microsoft area with this command:

GO MSEDCERT

MICROSOFT NEWSGROUPS

By pointing your Internet news-reading software to the NNTP news server at Microsoft, you can read ongoing news, questions, answers, and comments on dozens of topics close to Microsoft products.

Microsoft Public NNTP server: msnews.microsoft.com

Two typical hierarchies for your attention are:

microsoft.public.windowsnt
microsoft.public.inetexplorer

THE SALUKI E-MAIL MAILING LIST

Saluki is a very active majordomo Internet e-mail mailing list. Some days have 50 to 100 messages about MCSE studies and related topics. To subscribe, send an e-mail message to:

majordomo@saluki.com

In the body of the message write:

subscribe mcse Yourfirstname Lastname

For example:

subscribe mcse Scott Armstrong

You may use an alias if you wish. For further information about Saluki, write to Scott Armstrong at <saluki@gate.net> or Dean Klug at <deano@gate.net>.

PART ONE

Parts Is Parts

To master the Networking Essentials exam, you'll need to recognize and understand the fundamental components, structures, and operations of commonplace networks. This means you'll be required to be familiar with many terms and concepts associated with networking. You'll also be required to recognize and correct common misunderstandings, and to troubleshoot routine problems based on the visual and written vocabulary of networking.

You must know the terms to understand the concepts, so our Networking Essentials studies begin by summarizing the basic elements of networking that you'll need to pass the examination by providing extended definitions and examples of common networking situations and configurations.

First, in Chapters 2 through 4, we look at local area networks, then at the many telecommunication transport media available today, and then we'll consider the largest networks: wide area networks.

The other major parts of this book are:

Part Two: *Network Models.*   In Chapters 5 through 7, we discuss what's involved in peer-to-peer and client/server networking;

Part Three: *The Big Picture.*   Chapters 8 through 14 cover the OSI reference model of computer communication, several domain models, and the common protocols and topological structures of networks.

Part Four: *Implementation.*   In Chapters 15 through 18, we discuss administration of users and resources on networks, as well as hardware installation and troubleshooting and node addressing.

Part Five: *Keeping It All Running.*   Finally, Chapters 19 through 22 cover network monitoring, network diagnostic tools, network troubleshooting, fault tolerance, and disaster recovery.

CHAPTER 2

LAN Components

The smallest networks Microsoft includes on the exam are called *Local Area Networks* (LANs). We'll begin by defining components of a LAN:

Computer

Host computer

Computer network

Devices

Node

Protocol

Interoperability

Server computer

Client computer

Network standards

Proprietary standards

Point-to-point communication

Broadcast communication

Asynchronous communication

Synchronous communication

For clear communication to occur, we all need to be working from the same terminology, and we must agree on the meanings of words used. The following definitions lay the groundwork for our discussion of Networking Essentials in the rest of this book.

Computer.   An electronic device with its own operating system software. Also called a *host* or *workstation.*

Host computer.   A generic networked computer. Because it is a computer, it has its own operating system; and because it is networked, it must also have a network interface card (NIC) or another similar device to connect it to the network. On the exam, the word *host* always refers to a networked computer. The term *host* does not refer to the network role of that particular computer—the word *host* can refer to a server computer, a client computer, or to a peer-to-peer connected computer.

TIP
On the exam, a *host* computer can be a server computer, a client computer, or a peer-to-peer connected computer. The term *host* doesn't indicate the role of the computer. For the exam, remember that a *host* is a generic networked computer, not necessarily a server or client.

Another term used almost interchangeably with *host* computer is *workstation* computer. The term *workstation* does begin to indicate the role of that *host* computer, of course.

Computer network.   A collection of computers and other devices capable of communicating with each other using one or more common communication protocols over one or more common network transmission media.

Devices.   Any generic entity connected to a computer network may be referred to as a network *device.* Devices are often subdivided into two categories: *local devices* and *remote devices.* *Local devices* are physically present and visibly attached to and part of the network, or they are made available to the network through a networked computer that shares the device with users of the network. *Remote devices* are not physically present, but are similarly connected to the network or a remote networked computer.

The term *device* includes all the electronic equipment that comprises the network: client computers, printers, server computers, repeaters, bridges, switches, routers, etc.

Node.   All network structures may be thought of as a collection of *nodes* strung together with wires or some other network communication media. So, a *node* is another generic term for a device on a network. *Node* usually refers to a device that is an integral part of the network. (See Figure 2-1.)

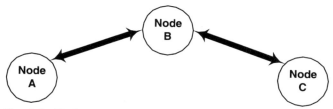

Fig. 2-1. Nodes A, B, and C are connected by a communication media carrying data from Node A to and from Node B, and to and from Node B to Node C.

Protocol. A language or set of communication rules and expectations used for the orderly transfer of information among computers. For two computers to communicate, they must have at least one communication *protocol* in common.

Interoperability. A product's ability to communicate with the products of other manufacturers over a network. Network standards have greatly enhanced *interoperability* and compatibility among various network devices.

Server computer. Generally, servers provide services and access to resources for client computers.

Client computer. Requests resources or services from server computers; servers provide these services to the requesting clients.

Network standards. Apply to communication protocols, network architecture, hardware interfaces, and other elements of communication networks. Product interoperability is often enhanced by the development of new network standards. *Network standards* are created formally and informally in a variety of ways. Formal standards organizations that have defined written procedures for standards development are listed in the sidebar "Network Standards Organizations."

Network standards are prone to a relatively short life cycle, because computer technology can change so rapidly that the standards process cannot predict changes well enough to keep up. Although open standards tend to promote interoperability, standards do not promise interoperability; and closed standards can actually be perversely used to prevent interoperability. Standards do tend to freeze technology in the past, at least briefly.

Proprietary standards. Some standards are closed and *proprietary* (not in the public domain), such as the standard for Novell's IPX/SPX protocol, or the standard for Microsoft's NWLink protocol. These standards may be used and accepted by only a limited number of specific hardware and software vendors. *Proprietary standards,* therefore, may lock customers into a relationship with only certain vendors.

NETWORK STANDARDS ORGANIZATIONS

By becoming familiar with and active within these organizations, you can participate in the standards setting process, if the process is open to citizen input. Check with your professional organizations for further information, or visit these Web sites:

Single-Country Standards Organizations

American National Standards Institute (ANSI)
   http://web.ansi.org/public/ref_lib.html

Association Française de Normalisation (AFNOR)—France
   http://www.afnor.fr/

Australian Communications Authority (ACA)
   http://www.austel.gov.au/

British Standards Institution (BSI)
   http://www.bsi.org.uk/

German Institute for Normalization (DIN)
   http://www.din.de/frames/Welcome.html

Norges Standardiseringsforbund (NSF)—Norway
   http://www.standard.no/nsf/

Standards Australia (SAA)
   http://www.standards.com.au/~sicsaa/

Standards Council of Canada (SCC)
   http://www.scc.ca/

European Standards Organizations

European Committee for Standardization (CEN)
   http://www.cenorm.be/

European Computer Manufacturers' Association (ECMA)
   http://www.ecma.ch/

European Conference of Postal and Telecommunications Administration (CEPT)
   http://www.eto.dk/ceptectra/default.htm

European Telecommunications Standards Institute (ETSI)
   http://www.etsi.fr/

International Standards Organizations

International Electrotechnical Commission (IEC)
  http://www.iec.ch/

International Organization for Standardization (ISO)
  http://www.iso.ch/

International Telecommunications Union (ITU) formerly called the
  International Telegraph and Telephone Consultative Committee
  (CCITT)
  http://www.itu.ch/

The Internet Engineering Task Force (IETF)
  http://www.ietf.org/

Professional and Industry Standards Organizations

Electronic Industries Association (EIA)
  http://www.eia.org/

Institute for Electrical and Electronics Engineers (IEEE)
  http://standards.ieee.org/board/index.html

The Unicode Consortium
  http://www.unicode.org/

Point-to-point communication.   Point-to-point communication uses data transfer technology to send information from one computer directly to another, rather than relaying the data among several computers or peripherals. Point-to-point communication generally implies the use of wireless networking components rather than a typical wired LAN.

Broadcast communication.   Broadcast communication is the sending of data simultaneously to all of the computers on the network. The broadcast communication is intended to be received by all computers on the LAN.

Asynchronous   communication.   A   data   communication method that carefully signifies the beginning and ending of each character transmitted. In asynchronous communications, data can be transferred at any time by the sending node without the receiving node having any advance notification of the transfer. An asynchronous receiving node does not know when data are about to be sent, nor does it know how large the incoming message might be, so asynchronous receiving nodes must always be in a ready state. Most data terminals, dial-up connections, and local data links are set up for asynchronous communication.

Synchronous communication. A data communication method in which data exchange is based on ordered data rates and data sizes. Synchronous communication usually occurs between only two nodes. Each node monitors the other, so that the receiving node knows in advance when a new message is being sent by the sending node, etc. All data transmission and link conditions are closely synchronized between the communicating nodes.

Synchronous communication tends to be more expensive than asynchronous communication. The hardware used for synchronous communication is more costly due to special, built-in clocking mechanisms and related electronics. Precise timing allows synchronous communication to be more efficient because it avoids some of the administrative overhead inherent in asynchronous communication. And, therefore, synchronous communication allows more data throughput and better error detection.

Network Topologies

Network topology is the basic physical layout or overall design of a computer network. *Topology* can be thought of as the architectural drawing of network components with nodes and a data transport medium linking the nodes. Some network designs are very simple, and other networks are extremely complex. The networks shown in this book are stylized to make them simple to describe, as are the networks you'll see on the examination.

Two principal categories of network topology are described in the following: The first is the point-to-point communication network category and the second is the broadcast communication network category.

Point-to-point network topologies. A point-to-point network topology consists of nodes that can communicate only with adjacent nodes. The simplest point-to-point network consists of two connected nodes. In more complex form, a point-to-point network could consist of 10 or 1000 adjacent nodes, with each adjacent node connected to another adjacent node.

Data addressed to a single host moves from adjacent host to adjacent host until it arrives at its destination. A single message may travel through many hosts, or few, depending on the network layout.

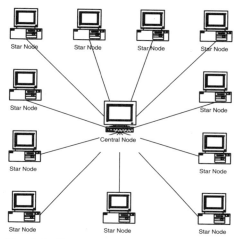

Fig. 2-2. Star point-to-point network topology.

There are several ways in which nodes can be linked together using a point-to-point design. These include star, loop, and tree topologies.

Note that a star topology is built around a single central node. The central computer becomes the most crucial part of the network—if it fails, the whole network is down, because all data must pass through the central node. (See Figure 2-2.)

Note that the loop network topology has no central node. The lack of a central node, and single point of failure, makes loop topologies generally more reliable than star topologies. The complete loop design is often considered one of the most reliable, and one of the most expensive, network topologies. See Figure 2-3.)

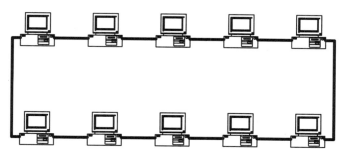

Fig. 2-3. Loop point-to-point network topology.

A tree point-to-point network topology has a hierarchical con-figuration. Note the "root" node at the top, with branches, and branches on branches. (See Figure 2-4.)

Broadcast network topologies. In a broadcast network topology, all hosts share a single communication medium. Unlike a point-to-point topology, data sent by one computer in a broadcast net-work topology is received by all other hosts connected to the network. Each host receives the transmission and inspects each message to decide if that message is addressed for that specific host. If the message is not addressed to this host, the message is discarded. Hosts in a broadcast network topology must use a spe-cial protocol or method for transmitting data so that only one node at a time can transmit.

Network broadcast messages can be categorized into three types:

Unicast messages are addressed to only one recipient host.

Multicast messages are addressed to a defined group of hosts.

Broadcast messages are intended for all hosts connected to the network.

In a bus broadcast network topology (see Figure 2-5), all nodes may transmit at any time, and all nodes hear each other's transmissions. Because two nodes theoretically may broadcast at the same time, a special method or protocol is needed for resolving such conflicts.

In a ring broadcast networking topology (see Figure 2-6), data travel around the ring. Some method is required to be sure that only one node can transmit data at any time. Data move from

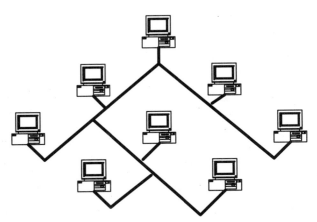

Fig. 2-4. Tree point-to-point network topology.

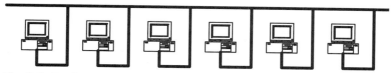

Fig. 2-5. Bus broadcast network topology.

source to destination by moving from node to node until the target node is reached.

Network Data Transmission Methods

Today, computer networks use many different data transmission methods. The following brief descriptions are oversimplified. Without these limited explanations, however, your understanding of network data flows might be found wanting.

Store-and-forward data flows. In store-and-forward networks, such as much of the traffic on the Internet, data are briefly stored at a sequence of intermediate nodes and then forwarded to the next adjacent node on the way to the destination node. Store-and-forward networks are characterized by their point-to-point basis, and by the fact that the entire contents of a packet must be received before it is forwarded to the next adjacent node.

Circuit-switched data flows. In a circuit-switched network, the path from the sending node to receiving node(s) is fixed and prearranged. Before any data are transmitted, a dedicated, switched circuit is created between the sending node and the receiving node. Once the data transmission is ended, the switch quickly tears down the dedicated circuit and that capacity is available to other nodes on the network. The Public Switched Telephone System is commonly described as a circuit-switched network.

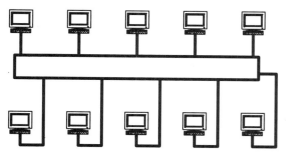

Fig. 2-6. Ring broadcast network topology.

Because of their ability to rapidly create and tear down large, dedicated data channels, switches are becoming increasingly popular and vital to LANs, WANs, to Intranets, and to the Internet.

Packet-switched data flows.   On packet-switched networks, many computers share one communication channel. To prevent any one computer or message from "holding" the channel all to itself for too long, ordinary messages are split into smaller messages called *packets*. Each packet contains only a few hundred bytes of data.

Each packet is also "self-sufficient" in that it knows where it is going, where it came from, how big it should be, and what its sequence number is in the larger message of which it is a small part. The source computer can send packets out one at a time, or in groups, at any time, and not necessarily in any particular order. In packet-switched networks, the packets are sent along the best route between the source computer and the destination computer.

After the network delivers all the packets to their destination nodes, the receiving computer reassembles the packets in correct order, and recreates the original message.

Packet and *datagram* mean generally the same thing. A packet is a series of bits formatted for transmission from one computer to another that contains data and control information. The packet header is the part of the packet that contains identifying information, length, source and destination addresses, and, sometimes, error-control data.

NOS: Network Operating System.   A NOS is the software for a network of computers that runs on a server and controls access to network resources. Typically, the NOS provides security and administrative tools. Banyan VINES, IBM LAN Server, Microsoft Windows NT Server, and Novell NetWare are all NOSs.

CHAPTER 3

Transport Media

This chapter discusses network transport media—cables. Copper cable is the most popular kind of network media, although the use of fiber-optic cable continues to grow. Both copper cable and fiber-optic cable are now commonly used in networks. For this exam, MCSE candidates are expected to be familiar with:

- Shielded and unshielded twisted-pair cable
- ThinNet and ThickNet coaxial cable
- Fiber-optic cable

The cable, also called the *physical medium,* carries the data signal over the network.

Cabling choices depend on the needs and requirements of a specific site. When selecting the type of cable to use on the LAN, some topics to consider are:

1. Installation logistics and requirements:

   How easy is the type of cable to work with and install?

   Are the distances the cable must cover long or short?

How stringent are network security requirements?

How many nodes are required?

How often will nodes be added?

Where will the cable be physically located?

2. Cost of the media:

What is the short-term cost of materials and installation?

What is the projected long-term cost of maintenance and upgrade?

3. Bandwidth: The amount of data transferred and the length of time required for data to be sent and received. Bandwidth is measured in megabits per second (Mbps).

How heavy is the anticipated network traffic?

What types of applications are supported on the network?

4. Transmission impairment—Attenuation:

 The degrading of a transmitted signal as the signal travels along the cable. As electrical signals travel along the cable, they weaken and become distorted. When cable length limits are exceeded, the signal may easily be lost.

What is the cable length limit specification?

5. Transmission impairment—Electromagnetic interference (EMI): A signal generated from an outside source causing electromagnetic noise that distorts the signal being transmitted on the network. Outside sources can include power outlets, motors, uninterruptable power supplies (UPS), and fluorescent lights.

How noisy is the environment where the cable will run?

Is cable shielding required?

6. Transmission impairment—Crosstalk: Occurs when signals from one wire become mixed with signals from an adjacent wire and create noise.

We begin to address these questions in this chapter. For further discussion, please see Chapter 11, "Designing Your Network Architecture."

Cables operate at the physical layer of the OSI reference model. The three primary types of cable media for the majority of networks are:

- Twisted-pair cable
- Coaxial cable
- Fiber-optic cable

Each of these cable types requires a different connector and a different port on the network interface card.

NOTE
A network interface card (NIC) is also known as a *network adapter card.* The NIC is the circuit board installed in one of the computer's vacant internal expansion slots that allows the computer to participate on the network. The NIC includes at least one port where the cable will connect. In today's market, a NIC is likely to support more than one cable type.

Twisted-Pair Cable

The usual twisted-pair cable is two strands of copper wire, each insulated, that have been twisted around each other. Twisting the wires around each other is an important characteristic of this type of cable. By twisting the wires, the cable's sensitivity to EMI and crosstalk is reduced.

Twisted-pair cable uses RJ-45 connectors. RJ-45 connectors, although similar to the RJ-11 connectors used with telephone jacks, have eight wires (or conductors), twice the number of wires in a RJ-11, and RJ-45 connectors are slightly wider than RJ-11 telephone connectors.

Twisted-pair cable has attenuation characteristics that limit cable length to a few hundred meters.

There are two types of twisted-pair cable—shielded twisted-pair (STP) cable and unshielded twisted-pair (UTP) cable.

Shielded Twisted-Pair (STP) Cable

Shielded twisted-pair (STP) cable has a higher-quality jacket than UTP and a foil wrap that functions as a shield between the wire pairs and around the internal twisting of the wire pairs.

STP is used less frequently than UTP, but has two advantages over UTP. First, STP is less susceptible to electrical interference. STP cable shielding provides comparable results to coaxial cable for EMI characteristics.

Second, STP can also support a higher transmission rate for a greater distance than UTP can. The STP cable used on Token Ring networks can have a data transmission rate of up to 16 Mbps.

Because STP is harder to install, less flexible, and bulkier than UTP, STP is much less frequently used. Also, although less expensive than thick coaxial cable or fiber-optic cable, the cost for shielded twisted-pair cables is more than for thin coaxial cable or unshielded twisted-pair cables.

And, like other copper-based cables, STP is vulnerable to electronic eavesdropping.

Unshielded Twisted-Pair (UTP) Cable

Unshielded twisted-pair wire cable (UTP) lacks the insulating shield found in STP, making UTP even more vulnerable to wiretapping.

Unshielded twisted-pair cables are the most susceptible to crosstalk and are more sensitive to EMI than STP cable, again, because the wires are not shielded. However, as long as caution is exercised when running the cable to avoid electrically noisy devices, UTP can be used in a large number of circumstances.

UTP cable is inexpensive to install and generally is the least expensive choice overall. (NOTE: UTP category 5 cable costs can be high because of strict installation procedures and the related special training needed for cable installers.)

Installation of UTP is relatively easy. Depending on the grade of UTP you choose (see sidebar), data rates range from 1 to 100 Mbps.

UNSHIELDED TWISTED-PAIR CABLE CATEGORIES

UTP cable is available in the following five grades, called *categories,* defined by the EIA/TIA (Electronics Industries Association and the Telecommunications Industries Association).

Note that category 1 and category 2 do not meet the standards for 10BaseT, discussed in Chapter 13, "Network Architectures on the Exam."

- Category 1 carries voice but cannot carry data. Category 1 was used in telephone wiring until the recent growth in the need for data-ready cables.

- Category 2 transmits up to 4 Mbps.

- Category 3 is the minimum category required to meet IEEE 802.3 specifications for 10BaseT and transmits data up to 10 Mbps. Most installation for telephone wiring is now done with category 3.

- Category 4 can transmit up to 16 Mbps. Category 4 has not developed market support. As an option between category 3 and category 5, the difference in performance is not a good economical choice.

- Category 5 is used in most new LAN installations. Category 5 supports a data transfer rate up to 100 Mbps. Category 5 is also the most vulnerable to crosstalk.

Coaxial Cable

Coaxial cable has several components. The inner copper conductor is surrounded with a dielectric material (insulation). A nonconductive outer layer surrounds the insulation. The inner conductor can be a solid core or a stranded wire core.

The outer insulating layer in the coaxial cable reduces the effects of EMI and crosstalk. However, coaxial cable is still vulnerable to electronic eavesdropping.

Both crosstalk and attentuation characteristics for coaxial cable are better than unshielded twisted-pair cable.

Coaxial cables have a characteristic electrical impedance measured in ohms. The impedance is determined by the diameter of the conductor and the opposition a cable presents to the alternating current.

Coaxial cable's bandwidth can range from a low of 2.5 Mbps on an ARCnet network to as fast as 10 Mbps on an Ethernet network.

There are two major types of coaxial cable used in computer networking: ThinNet and ThickNet.

ThinNet

ThinNet coaxial cable, although costing more than UTP cable, can be used for a greater distance. ThinNet provides somewhat greater security than UTP, and it is not as susceptible to interference.

ThinNet is easier to install than ThickNet because ThinNet is more flexible and is easier to connect to the network adapter card.

Configuration and installation are relatively easy and the cable is inexpensive.

ThinNet requires RG-58 A/U. RG-58 cable is available in different types. Be sure you use the correct type of RG-58 cable in the real world, and remember RG-58 A/U for the test, as well!

THE RG-58 FAMILY OF CABLE

Cable	Impedance
RG-58 A/U	50 ohms
RG-58 C/U	50 ohms
RG-58 /U	53.5 ohms

RG-58 A/U is the cable that meets 10Base2 requirements. 10Base2 networks are discussed in more detail in Chapter 13, "Network Architectures on the Exam."

RG-58 C/U is the military specification for RG-58 A/U.

The last version, RG-58 /U cable, contains a solid copper core and is used in cable television setups. Because RG-58 /U cable is cheaper than other coaxial cable, it is sometimes *incorrectly* used for Ethernet networks. You ought to use RG-58 A/U in real life, and on the exam.

ThickNet

ThickNet has a thicker core than ThinNet and a greater length limit. Commonly, a number of ThinNet network segments may be connected to the larger ThickNet cable being used as a network backbone.

COAXIAL CABLE AND FIRE CODES

There is another major difference between coaxial cables. There are two important grades of coaxial cables. Your choice of cable for your network will depend on the location of the cables in your office or factory.

Polyvinyl chloride (PVC) cable is the more common, and cheaper, cable grade. PVC is a plastic used in the cable insulation and jacket. PVC-clad cables can often be used in the open space of offices away from air handling ducts and equipment. However, when PVC burns, it releases poisonous gases.

Plenum-grade cable, on the other hand, contains fire-resistant materials and is less likely to release poisonous gases. Although plenum cable is not as flexible and costs more than PVC cable, there are cities, counties, and other geographic areas that require the use of plenum cable to meet local fire codes.

Plenum refers to the space, used for air circulation and wiring, above false ceilings and below raised floors.

Fiber-Optic Cable

Fiber-optic cable consists of extremely thin glass filaments enclosed in a sheath or jacket. These filaments, or strands, transmit signals of light. Because each strand can transmit a signal in only one direction, a fiber-optic cable has two strands in separate jackets—one strand for sending and a different strand for receiving.

Fiber-optic cable can carry large amounts of data for long distances at high bandwidths with low attenuation.

EMI is not a problem because fiber-optic signal transmissions are made with pulses of light—photons rather than electrons.

Fiber-optic cable also provides more security than copper cable because fiber-optic cable is almost impervious to electronic eavesdropping. Only the most determined and the best equipped of eavesdroppers can splice a fiber-optic cable without the network administrator noticing something.

Fiber-optic cable does have its disadvantages. Although in recent years the cost of cable and connectors has fallen, required electronic devices are still more expensive than their counterparts used with copper cable. And even with the reduced cost, fiber-optic cable is still the most expensive type of cable to install.

More training and specialized equipment is required to install fiber-optic cable. Fiber-optic cables require special care and attention during installation because the fiber can be easily damaged if the cable is bent too sharply or if the cable is stretched.

For Review

- There are three types of cable you're expected to know about:

    Twisted pair

    Coaxial

    Fiber optic

- There are two types of twisted-pair cable to remember:
  Shielded twisted pair (STP)
  Unshielded twisted pair (UTP)
- UTP uses RJ-45 connectors.
- There are two types of coaxial cable to remember:
  ThinNet
  ThickNet
- Fire codes sometimes require plenum-grade cable.
- Fiber-optic cable provides increased security over copper cables.

CHAPTER 4

WAN Components

Wide area networks are called *WANs* for short. This chapter is really an amplified glossary of the WAN parts and issues that MCSE candidates need to know to pass the Networking Essentials exam. Defining WAN components is somewhat more abstract than defining what goes into a LAN, as discussed in Chapter 2. This discussion of WANs is more abstract because WANs are much larger and, therefore, have more opportunities for variation between one WAN and another. This discussion is also more abstract because the exam is focused more on the conceptual facts about WANs rather than on day-to-day details that can be adjusted by network administrators. WANs contain everything and every combination of things under the sun! Fortunately, Microsoft doesn't expect you to know everything about WANs—yet, so save that for later.

Another term that is sometimes used for a network sized intermediately between a LAN and a WAN is metropolitan area network, or MAN.

The major WAN components which MCSE candidates should be prepared to deal with on the Networking Essentials exam include these:

ATM

FDDI

Frame relay

ISDN

PPP

SLIP

SONET

T1

T3

X.25

Most of this chapter discusses these large networking topics in alphabetical order, with a few more explanatory terms included as necessary.

WANS are typically too big, geographically, to have single-entity owners. Whether they be private networks of a large corporation, or of a government, WANs use many kinds of available transmission media, and in most cases parts of the WAN use public networks—common carrier transmission services.

Within a WAN, multiple links may be used to connect through two or three alternate transmission service networks to allow the assurance of connectivity, while also maintaining cost controls.

WAN design considerations include:

- Number of users in various parts of the organization
- Number of workstations and servers in various parts of the organization
- Resources required by different users and groups
- Bandwidth capacity and speed of each link of the WAN
- Budget available and projected
- Administration of network resources
- Security requirements throughout the network

Table 4-1 provides rules of thumb for how many users each of four technologies can support.

Asymmetrical Digital Subscriber Line (ADSL) is another telecommunication service possibly available from your local telephone company. Like ISDN, ADSL operates over copper wires. ADSL

Table 4-1. WAN Design Choices Are Often Based on the Number of Users.

Transmission method	Continuous connection?	Send/Receive speed	Users*
Analog modem	No	56.6 kbps	1–10
ISDN	No	128 kbps	10–500
T1	Yes	1.5 Mbps	50–500
T3	Yes	24 to 43.5 Mbps	Over 5000

* SOURCE: Microsoft Windows NT 4.0 Resource Kit, Supplement One.

requires a pair of special modems, one at your site and the other at the telephone company's site. The telephone company then connects the modem at their side to the Internet (not to the telephone system, see PSTN) with a router. ADSL is generally cheaper than ISDN for the telephone company to provide, and fast. Speeds up to 5 Mbps are possible, depending on the distance between your site and the telephone company site.

ATM

Asynchronous Transfer Mode (ATM) is an advanced CCITT standard for broadband packet-switched cell relay. It transfers data in small, fixed-length 53-byte cells rather than variable-length frames. ATM takes advantage of uniform frame size to switch, route, and transport data at enhanced speeds not practical with frames of variable sizes.

ATM Combines Video, Voice, and Teleconferencing

Microsoft is satisfied that ATM is appropriate for transmission of combinations of data, video, voice, and teleconferencing applications, and this knowledge is expected of MCSE candidates. ATM may be the ticket to richer, faster multimedia applications, and much is being invested in ATM's potential.

Large portions of the computer and telecommunications industries are working together to create ATM standards so that ATM is scalable and flexible enough to survive for many years after it is installed. ATM is intended to work well for both short-haul and long-distance network trunks, and for WANs with wide variations in numbers of attached devices.

Engineers like the efficiency of having all data transmitted on a single network, rather than having a completely separate network for teleconferencing, for instance. Obviously, having a single network also improves manageability.

ATM can use any transport media that offer appropriate physical interfaces. ATM can run as a layer on top of SONET (defined in the following) or other transmission technologies. The most common transport medium used with ATM is fiber-optic cable; however, twisted-pair and coaxial ATM options are available. Because ATM is not locked into a particular physical transport technology, ATM can be quite compatible with currently installed networks.

ATM is commonly configured in a star topology with a powerful switch in the center of the star to provide dedicated virtual circuits between sending and receiving computers.

ATM can transport WAN data at speeds much faster than Ethernet can. Everyday data transmission speeds of 155 Mbps and higher are available with ATM. The speed of ATM transmission is based on the line transmission technology being used, and ATM can be used with several. ATM implementations are available to transfer data at rates of from 25 to over 600 Mbps. Most Ethernet LANs today are limited to 100 Mbps at most, so use of ATM can open WANs to much higher data transmission rates.

ATM COSTS MORE

ATM network adapters and fiber-optic cable equipment are much more expensive than similar Ethernet fittings. Although the CCITT standard for ATM is open, ATM implementations can be proprietary. One reason there is so much effort to design ATM installations to be long-lived is because ATM is so expensive, it must stay in service several years to bring its life-cycle cost into a reasonable range.

To increase a network's effective bandwidth in the short run, some network administrators consider purchasing an Ethernet switch, which is more cost-effective than implementing ATM.

Another downside of ATM is that about 10 percent of every cell is devoted to overhead—every cell has a 5-byte cell header, and remember that every cell is a fixed length of 53 bytes.

ATM IS CONNECTION ORIENTED

In ATM, every cell traveling from the same source to the same destination travels over the same route. The switch in the center of the ATM star topology creates these virtual "connections" on demand. This makes ATM vulnerable to transitory network congestion and sudden surges in network traffic, and cells may be lost because ATM does not allow packets to take different routes to a destination, as TCP/IP does.

ATM ALLOWS YOU TO SET YOUR OWN PRIORITIES

ATM's promise is bandwidth on demand. But not all bandwidth is equal. Some data can endure a slight delay but must not lose a single packet. Other data can tolerate loss of a few packets but hate to be delayed. Audio and video data are in the second group, and file transfers are an example of the first kind of data. ATM allows you to set your own priorities by offering several billing and priority options.

- *Constant Bit Rate* (CBR) has a fixed bit rate so data travel in a constant stream.

- *Variable Bit Rate* (VBR) promises a specific throughput but data do not travel in a constant stream. Voice and videoconferencing data fit this niche.

- *Unspecified Bit Rate* (UBR) does not guarantee when data will travel. UBR is useful for applications, such as file transfer, that can tolerate delays. UBR is somewhat like standby airline travel—you go when they have available room for you.

- *Available Bit Rate* (ABR) promises a guaranteed minimum capacity and allows data to transmit at higher rates if network capacity is available.

CSU/DSU

As shown in Figure 4-1, *Channel Service Unit/Data Service Unit* (CSU/DSU) is the name of the last device before the phone company's line in most high-speed data circuits, excepting ordinary dial-up analog modems and ISDN. A CSU/DSU acts just like a modem, converting the computer network's digital signal to analog for transmission, and back again upon receipt.

Some CSU/DSU units work at a fixed rate, such as 56 kbps, and some work at a range of frequencies. It's important that the

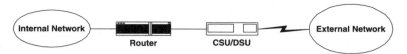

Fig. 4-1. Channel Service Unit/Data Service Unit.

router's capacity (bandwidth) match the CSU/DSU's bandwidth, and that the CSU/DSU and router are compatible with the hardware used in the external network. The CSU/DSU and router must also be designed to handle the transmission load on that WAN link.

FDDI

Fiber Distributed Data Interface (FDDI) is a high-speed token-passing ring network that uses fiber-optic transmission media, usually configured in a star ring topology. FDDI is commonly used in short runs near mainframes and minicomputers, for network backbones (for example, a segment of network that links several LANs together over a long distance or on a campus or in a large building), and for networks that require high data rates and abundant bandwidth, such as high-end corporate networks.

FDDI is an ANSI standard that calls for a 100-Mbps token-passing network. To provide built-in redundancy for fault tolerance, FDDI uses a dual counter-rotating ring architecture with two tokens circulating in opposite directions. Having two rings also allows more than one computer to transmit at the same time. Some installations use these fiber-optic networks for Ethernet today, in anticipation of using the fiber-optic backbone cables to carry FDDI in the future.

Each ring (of the two) used in FDDI is capable of accommodating up to 500 computers at distances up to 100 kilometers (62 miles). Optical fiber is used for many FDDI networks because fiber can transmit over greater distances than UTP cable.

Like Token Ring (IEEE 802.5), FDDI uses beaconing in ring troubleshooting. Beaconing is a complex process that automatically helps to isolate problems on a ring. When a device on the network encounters a serious error, it begins the beaconing process to help localize the problem by transmitting a beacon. Through a process of elimination, the computers of the ring network eventually identify the location of the problem.

Frame Relay

Frame relay is an advanced packet-switching technology based on X.25. It transmits data faster than X.25, because several portions of X.25 overhead were removed from its design. Frame relay uses switched private virtual circuits (PVCs) to transmit frames of variable sizes. It can be configured for bandwidth on demand. Some routers can handle frame relay, and others cannot.

ISDN

Integrated Services Digital Network (ISDN) is a digital telephone technology based on regular copper telephone wire. One ISDN line, with data rates up to 128 kbps, can support a half-dozen or more users, depending on the applications in use. ISDN was intended to completely replace the analog telephone system with a fully integrated, entirely digital system.

ISDN is commonly configured as a basic rate interface (BRI) or a primary rate interface (PRI). A BRI consists of two B (bearer) channels at 64 kbps and one D channel (for call set-up and take-down and other call management signaling) at 16 kbps. A PRI provides 23 individual 64-kbps B channels and one 64-kbps D channel.

Configuring routers for ISDN requires specific details supplied by the telephone company, such as the ISDN switch type and one or more service provider identifications (SPIDs).

Some implementations of ISDN BRI allow bonding of the two B channels to effectively achieve one wider channel. Also, some telephone companies will allow a kind of ISDN bandwidth on demand—you pay less for only one B channel, unless you need the extra capacity. In this case, when the second B channel is needed, the software dials and establishes another connection, and closes the connection when it is unused. Although the hardware and software to implement it is less available and more difficult to configure, it is also possible to use one B channel for voice communications and the other for data, simultaneously.

Packet-Switching

Packet-switching networks divide data into packets and transmit them to their destinations, where the data is reassembled from the packets. Switching refers to the action of switches in creating virtual circuits to transmit the packets toward their destination.

POTS

Telecommunications lingo for "plain olde telephone service."

PPP

 Point-to-point protocol (PPP), in cooperation with the TCP/IP software on a user's computer, together manage the connection and oversee the movement of data packets between the Internet or other external network and the user's computer over a dial-up connection with a modem. PPP offers enhanced security and other optional advantages over SLIP, and quickly replaced SLIP once PPP software became widely available. The technical advance provided by PPP that MCSE candidates are expected to know is that PPP allows software to *automatically assign* the remote (user's) computer a temporary IP address for the duration of that dial-up session, unlike the previously popular protocol—computers running SLIP don't know what their temporary IP address is. (see SLIP).

PSTN

Public-switched telephone network—the phone company's network.

SLIP

 Serial Line Internet Protocol (SLIP) was once used with TCP/IP over a modem to simulate a direct connection to the Internet. After the connection was made, the service provider would typically assign the user's computer an IP address for the remainder of that session, but there was no mechanism in SLIP for the user's computer to know what IP address was assigned to it. Complicated login scripts outside of the SLIP protocol were developed to retrieve the IP address for use after it was remotely assigned, but ordinary users were not expected to modify and configure these scripts, and this method did not proliferate after PPP emerged to replace it.

SMDS

Switched Multimegabit Digital Service (SMDS) is similar to ATM, and it is available from some local exchange telephone networks.

Using the same fixed-length cell relay technology that ATM is based on, SMDS is a switching service that provides high-speed one-way communication especially for multicast programs (for example, video broadcast programs transmitted from one point to many simultaneous remote users).

SONET

Synchronous Optical NETwork (SONET) is an ANSI standard for fiber-optic technology that transfers data at as much as 1 gigabit per second, or more, so SONET networks are quite capable of delivering voice, data, and video. SONET was developed by Bellcore for long-distance telephone applications.

T1

T1 is an AT&T term for a digital transmission line used for a Digital Service 1 (DS-1)–formatted digital signal at 1.544 Mbps. Overhead on a T1 line uses 8 kbps, so the usable bandwidth of a T1 circuit is 1.536 Mbps. You can't get your 1.536 Mbps of T1 throughput without buying a 1.544 Mbps line.

Depending on the application traffic involved, a single T1 line can handle 100 to 500 users. T1 lines typically have adequate capacity to carry both voice and data simultaneously.

As you have probably noticed by now, the fundamental building block of WAN data transmission technology is a 64-kbps line. How did this come to be?

Telephone companies are in the business of transmitting voice over copper and fiber lines. They found it expedient to transmit digital signals, although voice communications are analog in nature. Therefore, at each end of the communication path, a signal conversion occurs—first analog-to-digital, then digital-to-analog, and so on.

To recreate a "telephone-quality" voice sound at the far end of a circuit, engineers found that they needed to generate 8 bits of digital data 8000 times per second from the sending unit. This (8 × 8000) is the source of the standard voice transmission of 64,000 bits per second. So, in telephone networking, the basic 64-kbps channel is called a *DS-0*. Table 4-2 shows the multiples of DS-0 that are sold by telecommunications companies.

The phone company originally intended T1 to mean DS-1 delivered on a copper wire, and T3 to mean DS-3 delivered on

Table 4-2.
Digital Service Levels Are All Multiples of 64,000 bps.

Service	Multiple	Bandwidth
DS-0	1 DS-0 channel	64 kbps
DS-1 aka T1	24 DS-0 channels	1,536 kbps
DS-3 aka T3	672 DS-0 channels	44,746 kbps
E1 (European)	32 DS-0 channels	2,048 kbps

copper wire. That meaning has shifted so that people now refer to any link with the same bandwidth capacity as a T1 line or T3, although they are not necessarily delivered on copper wire.

Fractional T1

If you install a T1 line to a site, you don't have to use it all. Fractional T1 allows you to install the whole thing, but you save money by using only part of it. Later, if you need more capacity, you have part of it already installed.

Fractional T1 circuits are available as 128- or 256-kbps lines, or any other multiple of 64 kbps between DS-0 and DS-1.

A T1 line can similarly be used to deliver an ISDN PRI.

T3

T3 is a digital transmission line (the phone company likes to call it a *carrier facility*) used to transmit a DS-3–formatted digital signal at 44.746 megabits per second. T3 has 28 times more capacity than T1. (See T1.)

X.25

X.25 is a suite of protocols for packet-switching networks and is the oldest WAN switching method. X.25 networks use switched circuits to best route data based on current network conditions. X.25 was created to connect dumb terminals to mainframe computers, and requires error-checking overhead and special packet assemblers and disassemblers to connect to the network.

For Additional Information

Ascend Communications, Inc. Resource Library
http://www.ascend.com/169.html

Bay Networks Service and Support Library
http://support.baynetworks.com/library/index.html

The Broadband Guide Newsletters and White Papers
http://www.broadband-guide.com/news.html

ISDN to the Internet: A User Guide
http://www.ascend.com/1097.html

Michael Lamb's Frame Relay Stuff
http://www.best.com/~boober/links.html

Microsoft Network Communications for Windows & NT Server
http://www.microsoft.com/communications/

Routing and Remote Access Service Update for Windows NT
Server 4.0
http://www.microsoft.com/communications/routing&ras.htm

Virtual Private Networking and the New Windows 95 PPTP
client
http://www.microsoft.com/communications/pptp.htm

PART TWO

Network Models

When designing a local area network (LAN), you first determine the type of network to create. The two options we will discuss at length, because they are popular and also covered in the exam, are the:

Peer-to-peer network model

Client/server network model

Some of the essential items to be considered in designing networks are:

- Number of users in various parts of the organization
- Number of workstations and servers in various parts of the organization
- Resources required, and desired, by different users and groups
- Budget available and projected
- Administration of network resources
- Security requirements throughout the network

The information covered by the chapters in Part Two includes:

Chapter 5, "Peer-to-Peer Network Model," which lays the foundation for what you need to know about Windows 95 networks and Windows NT 4.0 workgroups.

Chapter 6, "Client-Server Network Model," which explains the many advantages of server-based networks, highlighting Windows NT 4.0 as a worthy server-based network operating system choice.

Chapter 7, "Access and Security," which covers both share-level and user-level security issues that are commonly covered in the Networking Essentials exam.

CHAPTER 5

Peer-to-Peer Networks

Peer-to-peer networking is the simplest and smallest of network types.

A peer-to-peer network is a popular choice when a small number of computers are being used for a common purpose, and the computers or users need to share mutual resources quickly and easily. Two to ten computers in close physical proximity can function reasonably well as a peer-to-peer network. As said in the caption to Figure 5-1, typical examples of peer-to-peer networks include networks comprised of computers running Microsoft's Windows for Workgroups (not pictured), Windows 95, and Windows NT Workstation, as well as networks running only other, non-Microsoft network operating systems (NOSs), such as AppleTalk, LANtastic, and Novell's Personal NetWare.

A peer-to-peer network may also be called a *workgroup*. In fact, Microsoft does call Windows 95 and Windows NT computers configured in a peer-to-peer network a *workgroup*.

In a peer-to-peer network, each computer in the workgroup functions as both a client workstation and a server. The peer-to-peer network model is sometimes implemented in an environment where the workstations all have adequate processing muscle, memory, and file storage resources to provide network server func-

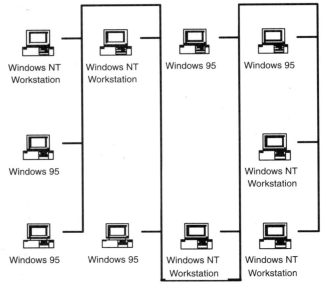

Fig. 5-1. Computers running Windows for Workgroups, Windows 95, or Windows NT Workstation can participate on the same peer-to-peer network.

tionality, or in environments where the cost of dedicating an entire computer as a server is considered prohibitively high. The peer-to-peer model is considered more simple, more versatile, and less secure than the client/server model because all workstations can directly access the shared resources of other workstations.

Resources that can be shared in a peer-to-peer network include files, printers, CD-ROMs, and other peripherals attached to any workgroup computer.

As said, peer-to-peer networks enable each workstation to directly access resources that have been shared on other workstations, without going through a centralized control point or server. For example, in Figure 5.2, workstation A is a client when accessing files located on workstation B's floppy drive. Workstation A is the server when workstation C sends a print job to the shared laser print device connected to workstation A.

Cost Savings

Peer-to-peer networks can cost less to implement and maintain than a server-based network because there is no need to purchase a dedicated server computer with server operating system soft-

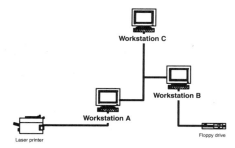

Fig. 5-2. Workstations can be both clients and file servers on a peer-to-peer network.

ware and client licenses for each client. And, because there is no centralized management or security, hiring a skilled, dedicated, and highly paid network administrator is not necessary.

Peer-to-Peer Management— One User at a Time

On a peer-to-peer network, each computer must be managed individually. Each user is responsible for the resources on one computer. The success of the workgroup as a whole, or of other members of the workgroup, can be compromised if one user in the workgroup fails to act in the best interests of the workgroup or of fellow users. Because any user on the network can access any shared resources on any workgroup computer (unless the resource is password protected), both scheduling and security on a peer-to-peer network must be handled carefully.

Because in peer-to-peer networks users function as "network administrators" for their own machines, it is essential that each user understand the importance of shared resources connected to his or her computer. Users must also have some understanding of how the peer-to-peer network works to avoid possibly incapacitating the network or unnecessarily preventing access to shared resources. In practicality, this means some users must be told, and perhaps reminded, to *never* turn off (or reboot) their computers while others might need access to connected or shared resources.

No Centralized Security

Peer-to-peer networks also have no centralized security. Access to resources is based on a password rather than an authenticated user account. Generally, peer-to-peer networks use share-level security, which is less powerful than user-level security. See Chapter 7 for more information on user-level and share-level security.

> **TIP**
>
> When Windows NT Workstation is configured as a member of a workgroup, it functions on a peer level. This means that an NT Workstation can be either a client or a server for the workgroup. As with other computers on the peer-to-peer network, resources and security on the NT Workstation are managed by each user of the computer—not in a centralized location or by a network or security administrator, unless the special Microsoft security enhancements for peer-to-peer networking are enabled.

Peer-to-Peer Windows NT Workstation Security Enhancements

There are several enhanced security features available in Windows NT Workstation computers when they are deployed in a workgroup environment.[1] Microsoft recommends that a local account should exist on each workstation for remote administrative access. They also mention that Windows NT "peer-to-peer networking features" should be enabled on the workstation. The cited article specifies that the administrative shares of the logical workstation drives C$ and ADMIN$ must not be disabled, and that the "everyone" group should not be removed from workstation user rights.

[1] "NT Server Product Facts: Novell Workstation Manager Technical Issues and Beyond." Microsoft's *TechNet* 5, no. 5 (May 1997).

CHAPTER 6

The Client/Server
Network Model

A Server-Based Network

If your network has more than 10 users, a server-based network is an important option to consider. A server-based network can be expanded to support thousands of users and workstations.

On a server-based network, servers manage the interactions between the client computers. Resources on a server-based network can be administered centrally, and a network administrator of some kind is required to administer and manage the centralized operations of the network. (See Figure 6.1.)

For example, a Windows NT 4.0 Server maintains a centralized database of user accounts and security information. Access to network resources is administered and controlled by the server. At the time a user logs onto a networked client computer, the server verifies the user account name and password prior to allowing access. See Chapter 7, "Access and Security," for more information on user-level security.

Unlike in the peer-to-peer networking model (discussed in the previous chapter), in a server-based network a particular computer will not usually be both a client workstation and a server at the same time. Client computers remain clients, and servers are exclusively used as servers in a server-based network.

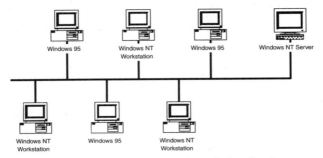

Fig. 6-1. A server-based network, also called a *client/server network*.

The cost to implement and maintain a server-based network is generally higher than the smaller peer-to-peer network. Servers have different and more substantial hardware requirements than client computers. CPUs, random access memory (RAM) chips, and hard disk drives purchased for servers must provide the server the capability to respond quickly to multiple simultaneous requests from the client computers.

TIP
If a Microsoft Windows NT network will include Macintosh client workstations, a peer-to-peer network is not an option because a server-based network is required. The protocols necessary for Macintosh computers to participate on a Microsoft network are not available unless there is a Windows NT Server on the network.

Windows NT networks, if they include a single server (either a primary domain controller, a backup domain controller, or even a member server), are another example of a typical client/server network.

A CLIENT/SERVER NETWORK

A client/server network is an efficient way to divide tasks between two computers:

- The client that sends requests to the server
- The server that processes requests from clients and returns responses to them

The client is also referred to as *the front end,* while the server is referred to as *the back end.*

Two applications that lend themselves well to the client/server network model are:

■ Database management on an application server

■ Centralized file storage on a file server

For example, a query is formulated and sent from the human user at a client computer to the server. The server processes the query and returns the results to the client.

NOTE: On a peer-to-peer network, all computers can be both client and server, usually simultaneously.

Server Types

APPLICATION SERVER

An application server is a computer assigned to perform a specific function or service, such as database management or message communication, on the network. An application server responds to client requests. For example, SQL server, a relational database, processes client queries and sends the results of the queries back to the client computer(s). The processing power resides on the application server, and the client computer merely places requests and receives replies.

FILE SERVERS AND PRINT SERVERS

A file server or print server provides a central location for file storage or printing. A file server or print server centralizes and maintains resources (files or printers) that are shared among users of the network. When a client computer requests a file from the file server, the server allows a copy of the file to be made on the client computer. The user then has the ability to work with that file using tools that are located on the client computer. The point is, a file server doesn't provide applications or processing power, it only provides access to files. Similarly, a print server might provide access to one or more special print devices, but a print server would not be expected to provide applications or processing power as an application server would.

CHAPTER 7

Access and Security

F or the Networking Essentials examination, there are two security models that you should understand:

1. Share-level security

2. User-level security

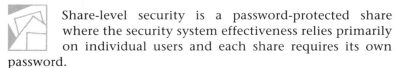

Share-level security is a password-protected share
where the security system effectiveness relies primarily
on individual users and each share requires its own
password.

User-level security is based on individual access permissions. Security is centralized with each user having only
one unique username and password. Permission to
access a resource is granted to individual users or, preferably,
groups of users. User-level security is preferred because of its ease
of use, administration, and because it is more secure—fewer people have actual administrative authority over resources, and
nobody has to remember passwords other than their own.

NOTE
A share is a resource somewhere on the network that users can access remotely. For example, a share can be a directory containing files or a peripheral device attached to one computer.

Share-Level Security

Peer-to-peer networks use share-level security. With share-level security, each user controls (and provides security administration for) the resources on his or her own computer. The user assigns a password to the resource so that other users may access the shared resource, if they are able to produce the correct password when they try to access the resource. The resource may also be open, so that anyone on the network may access the resource with no password at all.

With share-level security, any user who knows the password to a specific resource can access that resource at any time from anywhere on the network.

Security rests primarily with the users when using share-level security. Users may honor the security of network resources, or not. Users have even been known to turn off or reboot their computers when others still need access to a shared resource.

A Windows 95 network uses only share-level security. A Windows 95–only network cannot implement user-level security.

For example, on a Windows 95 network, a user wants to share information on his or her hard disk drive, making the whole drive a shared resource on the network. He or she can do this using Windows Explorer. After launching Explorer, right click on the drive to be shared. From the options listed select Sharing. A left click on Sharing brings up the screen in Figure 7-1. The default Access Type when a user clicks on Shared As: is Read-Only with no password entered. This allows all other users on the network read-only access to the drive.

There are three ways to grant access to a share in Windows 95:

Read-only

Full

Depends on Password

The user can now select the level of access to be granted on this share and choose whether to assign a password. If the Depends on Password option is selected, the user can assign two separate passwords: Read-only or Full access.

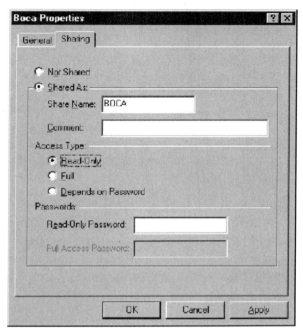

Fig. 7-1. A Sharing dialog box in Windows 95.

User-Level Security

User-level security on a Windows NT server-based network is implemented and maintained by the network administrator and is based on each user having a unique, individual username and a domain password. A Windows NT administrator can assign different levels of security access to each resource available on the network.

When a user or a group account is first created, the new entity is issued a security identifier (SID). Each SID is a unique machine-generated number created using information based on the user, time, date, and the domain that identifies the user or group account on that network. To determine the level of access to resources for a user or group, Windows NT Servers use the group's SID in place of a user or group's name. Each time a user attempts to access a resource, Windows NT verifies that the user's SID has been given permission to access the shared resource at the level requested.

User-level security access control is advantageous because it *does not* require a user to remember a separate password for each resource on the network. Network security and access to resources can be centrally administered and are not dependent on the memories of individual computer users.

To share a resource with Windows NT, right click the resource (share) in Windows NT Explorer. Select Sharing from the menu and click on the Shared As: option. When setting up the share, you can assign a share name, include a comment to clarify or amplify use of the share, and set a maximum number of users as shown in Figure 7-2.

After clicking the Permissions button on the Sharing dialog box, the Access Through Share Permissions dialog box becomes available. As shown in Figure 7-3, the Type of Access for specified users and groups can be set to:

- No Access
- Read
- Change
- Full Control

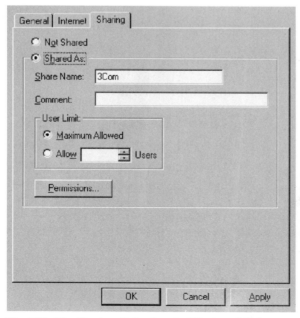

Fig. 7.2. The Sharing dialog box in Windows NT Server.

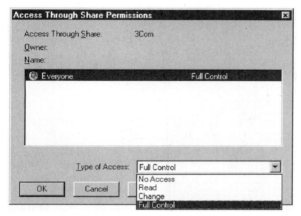

Fig. 7.3. Use the Access Through Share Permissions dialog box to set Permissions for shares on a Windows NT Server.

TIP
Windows 95 computers can employ user-level security if they are on a Windows NT server-based network.

For Review

- Share-level security allows each user to manage resources on an individual basis.

- Passwords are assigned to each resource in share-level security.

- Security rests with the user with share-level security.

- In user-level security, each user's unique username and domain password determine access to resources.

- Centralized security and management of resources are available with user-level security.

From Here

See Chapter 5, "Peer-to-Peer Networks," and Chapter 6, "Client/ Server Network Model," for more information on types of networks.

PART THREE

The Big Picture

Included in our discussion of each type of network architecture will be important items that must be considered and resolved to implement an appropriate network for a given situation.

Part Three includes domain models, the OSI reference model, and everything you need to know for the Networking Essentials exam about network topologies and network architectures.

Chapter 8, "Domain Models," covers the Windows NT 4.0 domain models available for small, medium, and large organizations.

Chapter 9, "OSI Reference Model," expresses and explains the classical networking communication theories that are embodied in this reference model.

Chapter 10, "Network Topologies," defines the fundamentals of the physical design or configuration of the computer network. It covers structure of the network and the layout of devices and cables.

Chapter 11, "Designing Your Network Architecture," discusses network standards that permit limited variation within specific rules and require particular hardware. Network architecture describes both the topology and the physical media of the network.

Chapter 12, "Network Topology Building Blocks," defines and elucidates the many connecting devices in today's computer networks—repeaters, hubs, bridges, routers, brouters, switches, and gateways.

Chapter 13, "Network Architecture on the Exam," focuses on the variations of Ethernet architecture and provides brief discussions of Token Ring and ARCnet network architectures.

Chapter 14, "Network Protocols," identifies various human-defined communication languages that computers on networks use to speak to each other.

CHAPTER 8

Domain Models

This chapter is about general models of relationships between computers in a Microsoft network. Just as large groups of people often arrange themselves into hierarchies, we also arrange large groups of computers running Microsoft operating systems into hierarchies on the network. Small groups of computers are also sometimes arranged in a peer-to-peer relationship.

In Microsoft networking, the computers at the top of the hierarchy are domain controllers. There are two types of domain controllers:

Primary domain controllers

Backup domain controllers

Both of these types of domain controllers run on the same Microsoft NT Server operating system (OS). The Microsoft NT Server OS is also used for two more types of servers on a network:

Member servers

Workgroup servers (also called *standalone workgroup servers*)

This chapter does not discuss the roles of other types of non-Microsoft servers that Microsoft networks also commonly include:

Novell servers

UNIX servers

and connections to various other non-Microsoft devices and services such as mainframe computers, IBM LANs, and network printers with their own network adapter cards.

This chapter does discuss how networks served by Microsoft Windows NT 4.0 Servers are arranged and controlled. As it happens, the Netlogon service is pivotal in explaining these different roles for NT Servers, and we therefore will introduce and briefly explain the Netlogon service.

When the Windows NT 4.0 Server software is installed on a computer, several crucial and some irreversible decisions must be made. You must decide, in advance, based on your network planning, whether you are creating

- A primary domain controller in a *new domain* (irreversible)
- A backup domain controller in an *existing domain* (irreversible)
- A member server
- A standalone workgroup server for a small workgroup

Are You Creating a Workgroup or a Windows NT 4.0 Domain?

How you organize the relationships between computers will impact resource availability and user productivity. Small groups of workers, say 6 to 10, can be easily networked with a workgroup, but important security and administrative features will be unavailable because workgroups are simply less secure and more difficult to administer.

The first thing we'll need to clarify, to show the differences between workgroups and domains, are the directory services structures they employ. There are two types of directory services structure supported by Windows NT:

Workgroup

Domain

The most powerful of NT's security and administrative features are unavailable when NT is used in a workgroup. For that reason, most network configurations will use one or another of these domain models:

- Single domain model
- Master domain model
- Multiple master domain model
- Complete trust domain model

After discussing workgroups, the remainder of this chapter explores the roles of Windows NT Servers, of the Netlogon service, and, finally, we cover the four domain models just mentioned. This chapter is for your initial understanding of Microsoft NT 4.0 networking, and builds a foundation for your study of Windows NT networking essentials.

Workgroups

A workgroup can be thought of as a loose association of computers without a central system of administration. Each computer's user is the administrator of that computer. As discussed in Chapter 5, "Peer-To-Peer Networks," sharing of resources is decided by each user and may be revoked on a whim or even by accident.

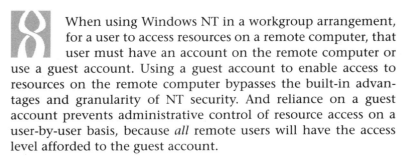 When using Windows NT in a workgroup arrangement, for a user to access resources on a remote computer, that user must have an account on the remote computer or use a guest account. Using a guest account to enable access to resources on the remote computer bypasses the built-in advantages and granularity of NT security. And reliance on a guest account prevents administrative control of resource access on a user-by-user basis, because *all* remote users will have the access level afforded to the guest account.

TIP
On the exam, if you encounter a question where you have *more than 10 computers* or need to have *centralized administration,* a workgroup is **not** the right choice. If a workgroup option is offered, you may consider it a distracter. By eliminating this obviously wrong option, you are closer to selecting the right option.

Why Choose a Workgroup?

As a rule, the workgroup organizational structure works well in a small office where the primary aim of networking is the sharing of a printer or a few files. As networks grow, workgroups are less attractive primarily due to the disadvantages already mentioned.

If a small organization is unable to spare the money to allocate even one computer as a dedicated server, a workgroup may be the appropriate directory service structure to use.

Another, more arcane use for a workgroup exists. If an NT Member Server (discussed later in this chapter) is needed in a remote domain, and access to the remote domain is unavailable at the time the Member Server software is being installed, a Member Server may be installed as a member of a workgroup as an expedient. Because NT Member Servers can be moved from one domain to another, changing the workgroup name to a domain name later will not be a problem.

TIP

Although NT Member Servers may be moved from one domain to another by simply renaming the machine in the Control Panel I Network Applet (on the Identification tab), primary domain controllers and backup domain controllers cannot be moved outside of their original domain. You can't even get them to join another domain with the *exact same name*. If a Windows NT 4.0 Domain Controller Server computer is needed in another domain, its Windows NT Server software simply must be reinstalled from scratch.

Microsoft uses several somewhat plausible descriptions on the NT exams to devise instances when you might want to move a domain controller computer from one domain to another, or to otherwise change its role to something other than a domain controller. These things cannot be done. When a domain downsizes or becomes defunct, all the domain controllers must go down with the ship. The only way to reuse an old domain controller computer is to reinstall the NT Server software in a new domain. More about this later in this chapter.

Domains

The two main advantages of using a domain model are for centralized administration of users and resources and a single, unified user logon.

Centralized administration provides easier administration *and* a more secure environment. The single logon allows users to access resources throughout the network without having to remember a separate username and/or password for each resource. In large and complex networks, this is an enormous advantage.

A domain is defined by its centralized directory database that stores user, group, and computer accounts. The domain database also contains security information, the role of each computer and user, and account properties. In Windows NT this vital database is referred to as the *Security Accounts Manager* (SAM).

Domain Controllers

The primary domain controller (PDC) computer has the authoritative copy and effective control of the SAM file. In fact, by installing a Windows NT Server in the role of the PDC, you create a new domain and the domain's SAM. The PDC has the only copy of the SAM that is both readable and write-able.

Because the PDC has the only editable copy of the SAM, the PDC has the responsibility of ensuring that the backup domain controllers (BDCs) have an up-to-date copy of the SAM. The BDCs each contain a read-only copy of the SAM that is synchronized periodically with the authoritative SAM that only the PDC may hold.

Although there can be only one PDC, there is no limit to the number of BDCs that may exist. The primary role of the BDC is user authentication. It is recommended that, to optimize user logon speed, another BDC should be installed for every 2000 users added to a network.

The PDC's primary function, on the other hand, is the maintenance of trusts with other domains, synchronization of all the domain controllers, and user authentication if the BDCs are overloaded.

If the PDC is ever not available (for example, because the network is down or the PDC is being rebooted), the BDCs will continue to validate user logons. However, changes cannot be made to the SAM because the BDCs have read-only copies of the SAM, so users will be unable to change their passwords, etc. If the PDC is unavailable, even administrators will be unable to

1. Create new user accounts
2. Create new groups
3. Add (or remove) computers to (from) the domain
4. Add or change domain policies

Also, while the PDC is not working, any resources usually available through trusts established with other domains will also be unavailable. (Trusts between domains are covered later in this chapter.)

TIP
If the PDC is offline, users cannot change their passwords and administrators cannot add or delete user accounts.

Likewise, if the PDC is offline, administrators cannot create or change user groups and policies, etc. They might as well go home, or to the golf links, until the PDC is back up, right?

Member Servers

 As mentioned earlier, not all Windows NT Servers are domain controllers. Windows NT 4.0 also allows two other kinds of server to be installed—the member server and the workgroup or standalone workgroup server.

Neither member servers nor workgroup servers ever receive a copy of the domain SAM database. They therefore cannot act as a logon server. Only PDCs and BDCs can validate domain logons.

Member servers do run the Netlogon service, but only to receive user account replications, not to act as logon servers.

Standalone workgroup servers cannot validate user logons for their workgroup and don't replicate user accounts, so they don't run the Netlogon service. Because standalone workgroup servers don't do user account replication, user account names and passwords may need to be changed manually on the standalone workgroup server.

RULES FOR SERVER ROLE CHANGES

There is much confusion about changing the role of a Windows NT 4.0 Server. Here is the most succinct way to understand the rules for server role changes.

Fact 1

A member server or standalone workgroup server can never become a domain controller.

Fact 2

A PDC or BDC can never become a member server or standalone workgroup server. *(You can even disable the Netlogon service causing a BDC server not to validate logins, but this does not change it into a member server—it's still a BDC in every other way.)*

Fact 3

- A BDC may be promoted to be the PDC for its domain. This action *automatically* causes the previous PDC to be demoted to a BDC as part of the process of promoting a BDC.

- Under normal circumstances, you cannot directly demote the PDC, you can only promote a BDC, which *causes* the PDC to be demoted.

Fact 4

You can rename a domain at the PDC, but it is still a different domain from any other domain, even other domains having the exact same name.

Fact 5

You <u>can</u> move a member server or standalone workgroup server between domains and workgroups.

WHY THESE FACTS ARE SO
Windows NT 4.0 uses *machine security identifiers* (SIDs) when construct-
ing a domain and the domain's security database. Because of these
machine and domain security identifiers—which are created at the time
of server software installation and cannot be changed—PDCs and BDCs
can't be moved from one domain to another without reinstalling the
operating system. This also explains why you cannot rename a domain
to merge it with another domain—even domains with the same name
have different security identifiers, and therefore cannot become one.
  Neither member servers nor workgroup servers ever receive a copy of
the domain SAM database, so they are able to move from one domain
to another without conflict between domain security identifiers.

Netlogon Service

The Netlogon service runs on every Windows NT workstation and
domain controller. The main function of the Netlogon service is
user authentication. In addition, the Netlogon service on the PDC
is also responsible for maintenance of trusts between domains.
Synchronization of the SAM for all domain controllers in the
domain is also accomplished through the Netlogon services.

User Authentication

Because user authentication is accomplished through the Netlogon service, users only need a single login account and password to provide access to all of the network's resources. On a
computer running Windows NT Workstation or Windows NT
Server that is not a domain controller, the Netlogon service is
responsible to process requests for access to that computer via the
Local Security Administration Subsystem (LSASS).
  If the request is to log onto a domain, the request is passed
through to the Netlogon service of a domain controller (either a
BDC or the PDC). This is accomplished in three steps:

1. A domain controller is located. This is accomplished either by
   broadcasting a request for domain controller services or by
   requesting a list of available domain controllers from a WINS
   server.
2. A secure communication channel is established between the
   computer making the request and the domain controller.
3. The computer sends the logon request to the domain controller to check account authentication. Once the account has

been identified as valid, the information is returned to the logon computer and the user gains access.

Synchronization

The Netlogon service is also responsible for synchronizing the SAM on the PDC with the read-only copies of the SAM that reside on all the BDCs. The PDC sends periodic notices to the BDCs that advise the BDC that it should request any changes that have been made to the SAM since the last synchronization. This interval is five minutes by default and can be altered by changing the Pulse frequency parameter in the registry of the PDC.

As changes are made to the SAM, they are noted in the change log. The change log is then used to determine if, and how, a BDC needs to be updated. When a BDC requests updates from the PDC, the change log is consulted to determine which changes should be sent to that BDC. By default, the change log can contain approximately 2000 changes before the older entries are overwritten.

A change log of 2000 entries is usually large enough to prevent the necessity of a full synchronization, which is more time and resource intensive and therefore undesirable.

Server Manager may be used to force synchronization if the administrator desires it. An administrator may select to either synchronize the entire domain or to synchronize a single BDC. This is helpful after you've made changes that you want to be available to your users.

Trusts

Often users in one domain need to access resources in another domain. Access to resources in multiple domains can be accomplished by creating a trust between the domains. A trust is a way to functionally combine the SAMs of two domains into one administrative unit. Trusts are used to authorize user access to resources in both domains.

Trusts are one way only. There is no surety that if domain A trusts domain B, then domain B will trust domain A. Administrators in both domains may establish two trusts—one in each direction, so that both domains do trust each other and have a two-way trust *relationship*. However, it takes two trusts—there is no such thing as establishing a two-way trust.

Also, access rights are not transmissible from a trusted or trusting domain. If the Research domain trusts the Marketing domain, and the Marketing domain trusts the Production domain, there is no "implied" or "pass-through" trust between the Research domain and the Production domain. Access permissions between two domains cannot be passed through to a third domain.

Figure 8-1 shows both the Corporate and Research domains as trusting the Support domain.

With this arrangement, users from the Support domain can access resources located in either the Corporate or the Research domain. However, users in the Corporate domain cannot access files located on a server in the Research domain.

When a user from Support (trusted domain) logs on from a computer in Research (the trusting domain), the request for authentication is forwarded to the PDC of the Research domain. Since that user does not exist in the SAM of the Research domain, the Research PDC forwards the authentication request back to the Support PDC using pass-through authentication. The Support PDC authenticates the user and passes this information forward to the Research PDC. The Research PDC then allows the user to log on.

Trusts in Windows NT 4.0 are created using the administrative tool menu program called User Manager for Domains. From the User Manager for Domains menu, select Policies/Trust Relationships. Figure 8-2 shows the dialog box used for configuring a trust. A domain administrator can designate whether one domain will trust another domain, and whether one domain will allow

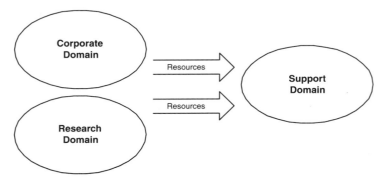

Fig. 8-1. The Corporate domain and Research domain are the trusting domains and Support is the trusted domain. The arrow always points in the direction that resources would flow, from the trusting to the trusted domain.

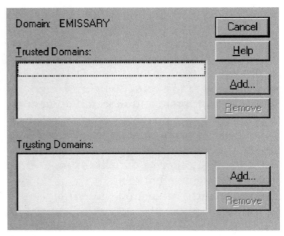

Fig. 8-2. Enter the name of either the trusted or the trusting domain.

another domain to trust it—trusts must be authorized from both sides. Each trust must be configured by the administrators of both domains before it is achieved.

Domain Models

Windows NT networks are fully scalable. Windows NT can be used to create large networks of many thousands of computers. Depending on the size of the network, administrators may choose various domain models to accomplish various administrative goals:

- Optimizing efficient use, distribution, and availability of resources
- Security, access control
- Fault tolerance
- Budgeting, financing, and controlling costs
- Innovation, version control, license control
- Expanding or shrinking network capacities

Microsoft considers all of these management issues important, especially because network managers have an immense and pivotal role in software and hardware purchasing decisions. Therefore, any MCSE candidate should expect to understand how these management issues are addressed by Windows NT features when an NT network is configured in any of several domain models.

First we'll consider the simple single domain model. Then we'll cover the master domain model, the multiple master domain model, and, finally, the old complete trust domain.

Single Domain Model

In the single domain model, there is one PDC that contains the authoritative SAM for that domain. The SAM contains all of the accounts, users, groups, and computers. One or more BDCs are used to assist with user authentication. The single domain model can contain up to approximately 26,000 user accounts as well as the associated group and computer accounts. Once the organization has grown past these 26,000 users, another domain model must be used. Figure 8-3 diagrams the Support domain, which is a single domain.

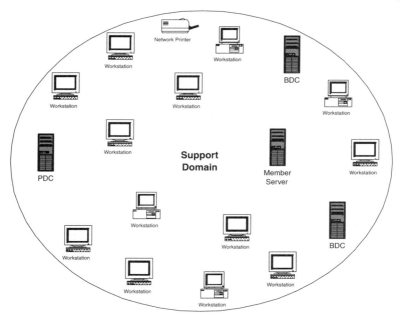

Fig. 8-3. The Support domain, a single domain, has one PDC that contains the SAM. One or more BDCs provide for faster login.

Master Domain Model

If an organization has outgrown the single domain model, then the master domain model may be implemented. With this model, all user accounts are contained in the master or account domain. Additional domains are created as resource domains. Each resource domain trusts the master domain and contains the computer accounts.

Users log on using a computer in one of the resource domains. The authentication request is passed through (via the trust) to the master domain PDC that approves the user's access. Figure 8-4 illustrates a master domain model.

Multiple Master Domain Model

If an organization spans multiple locations, it may be too cumbersome, or politically impractical, to have all account administration in one location. The multiple master domain model addresses this issue by providing for more than one master or account domain. The multiple master domain model also removes the overall limit of 26,000 users, as each new master domain can handle an additional 26,000 users.

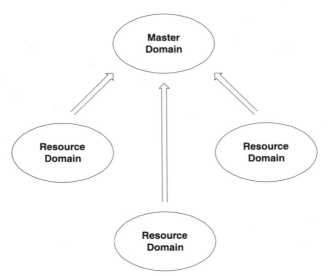

Fig. 8-4. The master domain model includes a master or account domain and one or more resource domains.

As in the master domain model, resource domains must trust the master domain. However, the number of trusts that must be maintained can increase significantly because each resource domain must trust each master domain. Figure 8.5 illustrates a multiple master domain model.

Complete Trust Domain Model

The most complex and difficult to maintain domain model is the complete trust. This model consists of two or more single domains that trust each other. As the number of domains increases, the number of trusts that need to be maintained also increases significantly. This model is sometimes used when divisions or departments want to have administrative control over users and resources but still need to share some resources. Figure 8-6 shows a diagram of a complete trust domain.

Because the number of trusts needed to maintain a complete trust domain grows rapidly as the network grows, and because the work of maintenance is increasingly demanding, Microsoft no longer recommends this model. If you encounter a complete trust domain model on the exam, it will likely be that you are to know

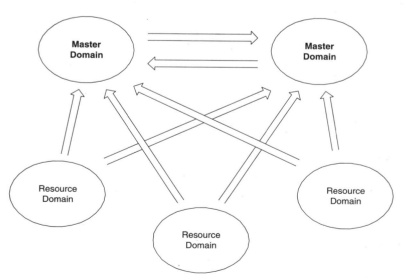

Fig. 8-5. The multiple master domain can contain two or more master domains and as many resource domains as are necessary.

106 **The Big Picture**

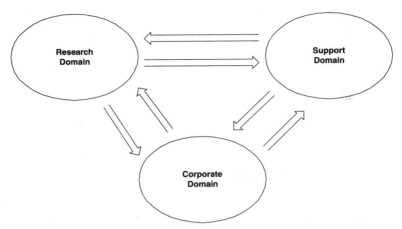

Fig. 8-6. The complete trust domain model consists of multiple single domains that trust each other.

that complete trust domains are undesirable and not the "best answer." The upkeep on complete trust domains rapidly becomes immense.

Your choice for organizing your network will be dependent on many factors, the most important being the type of network administration and security you wish to implement. Second, the number of users and computers will need to be considered. If the number of users is greater than 6 to 10, or if centralized administration is desired, one of the four domain models is a better choice than a workgroup.

For Review

- Workgroups are for 6 to 10 computers and users.
- Domain models allow centralized administration, enhanced security, and simplified access to shared resources.
- PDCs and BDCs cannot be moved to another domain—just reinstalled.
- Member servers *cannot* be promoted to domain controllers.
- Member servers can be moved between workgroups and/or domains.
- Plan for 2000 users per BDC.

- Plan a maximum of 26,000 users per domain for single domains and single master domains.

- Each trust is one-way and involves only two domains.

- Creating a trust requires action in both domains.

- The trusting domain grants access to its resources for users from the trusted domain—the arrow shows the direction that resources flow.

From Here

Chapter 5 discussed peer-to-peer networks such as Windows NT 4.0 for Workgroups. Chapter 9 discusses the OSI reference model of communication, and Chapter 11 talks about considerations for designing networks.

CHAPTER 9

OSI Reference Model

ISO/OSI Reference Model

The *International Organization for Standardization* (ISO) devised the set of specifications known as the *Open Systems Interconnection* (OSI) reference model. The OSI reference model was developed to define the rules of how communication occurs on a network.

The full, formal name for the OSI model is *ISO Basic Reference Model for Open Systems Interconnection* (ISO/OSI). The ISO/OSI model describes computer-to-computer communication protocols, without regard to the programming language, platform, operating system, application, or user interface involved.

The ISO/OSI model is a simple way of organizing knowledge about computer communication that provides the common basis for discussion. It is a layered model—with each layer providing defined functions and services and calling and relying on the services of other adjacent layers. Isolating services and functions into layers is intended to promote interoperability.

The OSI reference model is not a set-in-stone rulebook. The model provides a framework to help humans understand how communication occurs between two computers, even if the computers are using different operating systems and different hardware platforms. To aid in understanding, the OSI reference model includes detailed descriptions of what happens within each layer.

The OSI reference model is represented in seven layers. Each layer is responsible for a particular aspect of the computer-to-computer communication process.

The seven layers of the OSI reference model are shown in Table 9-1.

To pass this exam, you'll also need to know what goes on at each level of the Open Systems Interconnection reference model, not just the order that the model defines for communication processes. For the exam, note the kinds of processing that are done at each layer of the model and, finally, note which network devices are associated with each layer of the model.

Think of the Open Systems Interconnection reference model as a way of organizing all the detailed work that must be done for computers to communicate. The Open Systems Interconnection reference model helps telecommunications engineers and MCSE candidates remember the many sequential steps in the computer-to-computer communication process, omitting none, and performing each step in the process in the proper sequence.

Table 9-1. Open Systems Interconnection (OSI) Reference Model.*

From Top to Bottom	From Bottom to Top
1. Application	1. Physical
2. Presentation	2. Data Link
3. Session	3. Network
4. Transport	4. Transport
5. Network	5. Session
6. Data Link	6. Presentation
7. Physical	7. Application

* The Open Systems Interconnection (OSI) reference model is so important that you must memorize the sequence of the model for the examination. To aid your memorization, here are two (of the many available) mnemonics. Choose, or generate, a mnemonic that works for you, and remember it!

From Top to Bottom: ALL PEOPLE SEEM TO NEED DATA PROCESSING
From Bottom to Top: PLEASE DO NOT THROW SAUSAGE PIZZA AWAY

Although the Open Systems Interconnection reference model may not correspond well to the real-world equipment where you work (as compared to the similar TCP/IP model, for instance), the OSI reference model does correspond well to the several questions on the real Microsoft Networking Essentials Examination. Therefore, successful MCSE candidates take this model seriously and study it appropriately.

Physical Layer

The physical layer is the "lowest" or "first" layer. This layer defines how the physical transmission medium, the cable, is attached to the computer's network interface card (NIC) and what transmission technique is used to send the data over the cable. The physical layer is responsible for transmitting the bits of data from one computer onto the cable connecting to another computer. A bit is a unit of data represented in binary arithmetic as 0 or 1, OFF or ON.

Data Link Layer

Next is the data link layer. On the receiving computer, the data link layer assembles the bits of data received up from the physical layer into data frames. A data frame is a structured packet of data. On the sending computer, data frames are passed down from the network layer, by the data link layer, to the underlying physical layer, where the data frames become outgoing data bits and are no longer data frames. The receiving computer's data link layer is responsible to assemble the bits of data back into data frames, and to pass the frames up to the network layer.

The data link layer is sometimes broken down further into two layers: the media access control layer and the logical link control layer.

The data link layer also ensures that data is correctly received. If an acknowledgment of receipt is not received by the sending computer, or other transmission problems are detected, the data link layer of the sending computer is responsible to resend those frames.

Network Layer

The network layer is responsible for determining the physical route through the network for data transmission. Translating logical addresses and names into physical addresses occurs at the network layer. The network layer handles transmission problems on the network including congestion and packet switching.

Transport Layer

The next layer, the transport layer, handles error recognition and recovery, providing for error-free delivery. The transport layer also segments large messages into smaller packets needed for transmission by a particular protocol or network. Later, on receipt, the transport layer of the receiving machine reassembles the data into the original message and sends back a message acknowledging receipt of the message. Also, this layer provides additional flow control, error handling, and packet handling.

Session Layer

The session layer controls a communications session between two applications on different computers. It establishes, reestablishes, uses, and ends an exchange between the computer systems involved in a communication event. The session layer, using checkpoints placed in the data stream, synchronizes data transmittal. If there is a communication failure, the session layer retransmits the data that followed the last successful checkpoint.

The session layer is also responsible for user account name recognition, user authentication, and for performing logins and for controlling resource-access security.

Presentation Layer

That brings us to the presentation layer, which translates data into a final format usable by everyday applications. The presentation layer on the receiving computer translates the data into a format that can be used by the application layer on that computer. On the sending computer, the presentation layer receives data down from the application layer and translates that data into an intermediary format for sending on the network.

The presentation layer also handles data compression. By using compression, the amount of data (the number of bits) required to be transmitted on the network is reduced.

The presentation layer also provides data encryption. An example of data encryption would be the transmission of a specially formatted (encrypted) password so that those not intended to understand the data will not be as likely to be able to decode it.

Application Layer

The top layer of the OSI reference model is the application layer. The application layer is where you'll find services that are accessible by user software applications. Examples of user application software services that are supported at this level are transfer of files between two computers, access to network print devices, electronic mail, and time services.

For Review

Table 9-2. Activities and Responsibilities in the Open Systems Interconnection (OSI) Reference Model.

Layer	Activities and Responsibilities
Application	Services and procedures for user applications, file transfers, and e-mail
Presentation	Provides data compression, encryption, final formatting
Session	Opens and closes network communication dialog, retransmits on connection failure, synchronizes the flow of data, name lookup, and security functions
Transport	Provides error recognition and correction, assembly, disassembly, priority, sequencing, acknowledgement of receipt
Network	Routes logical addresses to physical addresses, provides packet resizing if needed, handles network congestion
Data Link	Translates bits to frames; frames to bits; provides flow control; replaces lost or damaged frames; handles error recovery
Physical	Defines physical connection to network media, transfers bits across the link

Devices for Each Layer of the Open Systems Interconnection (OSI) Reference Model

Repeaters

Repeaters work at the physical layer of the OSI reference model. Repeaters are used on a network to maintain the strength of a signal. As the signal moves away from its source, it tends to attenuate or lose strength. A repeater regenerates any signal that it receives and then forwards the signal on its way, thus solving any attenuation problem. Repeaters are fairly simply devices, comparatively, and their primary reason for being is to strengthen the incoming signal to return it to its original state, rather than modifying the signal in some other way. While a repeater can join different types of media, repeaters cannot connect media that use different protocols, different media access schemes, or different transmission techniques.

Bridges

Bridges work at the data link layer of the OSI reference model. A bridge joins networks into a logical network. A bridge can join different physical media or architectures.

A bridge can forward data to a location on the network via a specified route. If the sending and receiving addresses are located on the same section of the network, the bridge can reduce network traffic by *not forwarding* the data across the bridge. Bridges can create broadcast storms, by forwarding the data to all nodes, if the bridge does not know the destination address of the incoming data.

Because bridges function at the media access control sublayer of the data link layer, they are sometimes called *media access control sublayer bridges.*

Routers

Routers work at the network layer of the OSI reference model. The network layer determines the path the data takes as they move from the sending computer to the receiving computer. Routers aid in connectivity because they can connect networks that use different topologies. Routers can send data between different topologies because they remove and recreate the data link layer source addresses and destination addresses.

Routers can improve network performance because a router can select, and in many cases learn and remember, the best route for data to take in reaching a specific network address. Routers can curtail or eliminate broadcast storms because routers generally do not forward broadcasts.

Gateways

Gateways generally work at the application layer of the OSI reference model. Gateways are sophisticated, often powerful devices installed between different networks that require a translation of protocols, architecture, and/or data format. A gateway, usually a dedicated server, performs a specific translation on a network. For example, a gateway can perform the role of a post office and distribute electronic mail across different networks requiring several e-mail formats.

Some gateways can access all seven layers of the OSI reference model, so it is not enough to simply say that "gateways work at the application layer."

Brouters

Brouters combine components of a bridge and a router. While one transport protocol (for example, TCP/IP) uses the brouter as a router, other protocols might use the brouter as a bridge. For example, although the NetBEUI protocol is not routable, NetBEUI could use a bridge to cross into another part of the same network.

BROADCAST STORMS

A broadcast message must be processed in some way by each and every computer on the network. When too many broadcasts occur at the same time, it can prevent normal data communication. When the number of broadcast messages surpasses the ability of the network to transmit other messages, a "broadcast storm" is hindering the efficient functioning of the network.

For Review

Table 9-3. Network Devices Operating at Various Levels of the Open Systems Interconnection (OSI) Reference Model.

Layer	Network Devices Operating at This OSI Level
Application	gateways
Presentation	
Session	
Transport	
Network	routers, brouters
Data link	bridges, brouters
Physical	repeaters, network interface cards (NICs)

CHAPTER 10

Network Topologies

This chapter discusses network topologies. By definition, a network is a collection of computers and peripheral devices connected together, usually with cables, sharing hardware and software in common. The topology of a network is the physical design or configuration of the computer network. A physical topology model is a representation of the network structure and the layout of devices and cables.

A network also has a logical topology that can be different from or the same as the physical topology. The network logical topology represents the signal path on the network.

An example of a network with a logical topology different from its physical topology is Token Ring. A token ring network has a star topology configuration because each device is connected to a central device, usually a MSAU (*Multistation Access Unit*). The logical topology of a token ring network is a ring. A token ring network uses the token-passing media access method as defined by IEEE 802.5. (See Chapter 12, "Network Topology Building Blocks," for a discussion of media access methods.) The MSAU passes the token to each device in a predetermined sequence, allowing equal access to the network for each device. For further discussion of a token ring network, see Chapter 11. "Designing Your Network Architecture."

An example of a network with a logical topology the same as its physical topology is Ethernet 10Base2 (ThinNet). ThinNet's physical topology is a linear bus. ThinNet's logical topology is also a bus because the signal is common to each device on the cable. For further discussion of an Ethernet 10Base2 network, see Chapter 13, "Network Architectures on the Exam."

There are four basic types of network topology:

Bus

Star

Ring

Mesh

There are also two hybrid topologies derived from the above basic topologies that you should be familiar with:

Star bus

Star ring

Bus Topology

A bus topology (also known as *linear bus*) has a common, central cable; and each device connects directly to the cable as shown in Figure 10-1. Each device has access to the other devices on the network and can communicate directly.

A bus topology, although frequently used as a network backbone, is also appropriate for a temporary network or a small workgroup that has fewer than 10 computers. The initial installation cost of a bus topology network is low, and the installation process is relatively easy. A bus topology can provide the foundation of a simple and reliable small LAN.

A bus topology, however, can prove troublesome when the network needs to be reconfigured. And when additional devices are added to the existing cable, the network must be shut down while the connectors are being installed. This is one reason bus topologies are rarely used for new installations.

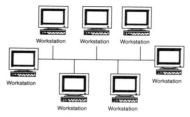

Fig. 10-1. A bus topology.

Another reason for their current limited use is that unless the LAN is small, a bus topology can be difficult to troubleshoot because there is no hub or central point. If one device fails or there is a break in the cable, the network can fail. Isolating the problem can be difficult and time-consuming.

A bus topology uses the CSMA/CD access method. Bandwidth can become an issue, because as traffic increases the network will slow down. As discussed in Chapters 11 and 12, "Designing Your Network Architecture" and "Network Topology Building Blocks," with CSMA/CD only one computer can transmit at a time. As computers are added to a bus topology, transmission speeds are reduced.

On a bus network, a computer will transmit a signal in both directions along the cable so that all other devices on the network can receive the signal. To stop a signal from bouncing, the two end points must be terminated. If transmissions were not terminated, other devices would never have an opportunity to transmit.

Star Topology

In a star topology each device connects to a central hub with a dedicated cable. One end of the cable is connected to the NIC on the device and the other end connects to a port on the hub. Figure 10-2 shows a star topology.

A star topology is easy to install and expand or modify. The network does not have to be shut down to add new computers. A centralized hub provides for relatively easy management of resources.

Because of the centralized hub, a star topology can be easy to troubleshoot. If one device fails, the other devices on the network generally are not affected. The hub can be used to isolate problems. Unfortunately, if the hub fails, the network fails.

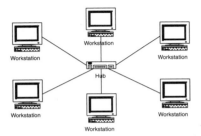

Fig. 10-2. A star topology.

 Because each device requires a separate cable connection to the hub, the cabling costs are higher for a star topology.

Another downside of the star topology is that bottlenecks can occur at the hub because all data must pass through the hub.

Ring Topology

In a ring topology, devices are connected in a ring or continuous loop on a cable, and there is no centralized device or hub. Each device is connected to two other devices in the circle. A ring topology is shown in Figure 10-3.

Data is transmitted from one device to the next device as the signal moves clockwise around the ring. Each device, acting like a repeater, regenerates the signal, so that if one device fails, the network fails.

 Ring topologies can offer a high bandwidth while providing each device with equal access to the network.

Also, a ring topology network can be installed with minimum difficulty.

Adding or modifying a device on a ring topology may interrupt network operations because the network might be required to shut down temporarily.

Mesh Topology

A mesh topology provides for a direct link between each and every device on the network. Figure 10-4 shows a mesh topology.

As the number of devices increases, installation and manage-

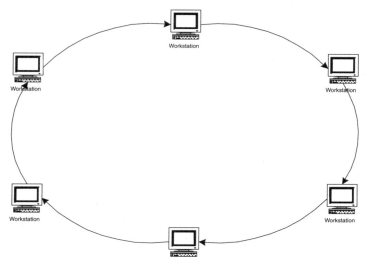

Fig. 10-3. Each device is connected to the devices on either side of it in a ring topology.

ment become more difficult. For example if your network contained 5 devices, 10 connections would be required. And if your network had 6 connected devices, 15 connections would be required. Seven computers would require twenty-one cables. So, for practical reasons, a mesh topology is primarily used in small peer-to-peer workgroups. In its favor, a mesh topology is easy to troubleshoot and quite fault tolerant. Because of the redundant links, data can be transmitted along different paths if one cable fails.

STAR BUS TOPOLOGY

The star bus topology is a hybrid topology combining elements of the star and bus topologies as shown in Figure 10-5.

Although the initial cost for a star bus topology will be greater than a bus topology, the maintenance costs will be less. A star bus allows for future growth and relatively easy reconfiguration.

If one of the computers fails, the network will not be affected. If one of the hubs fails, the computers connected to that hub will be unable to access the network until the hub is repaired or replaced.

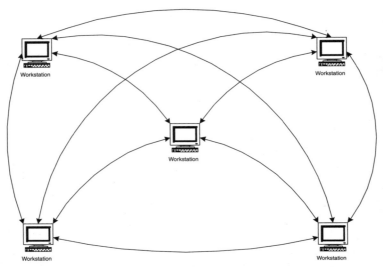

Fig. 10-4. Each device is interconnected with all of the other devices on the network in a mesh topology.

STAR RING TOPOLOGY

A star ring topology is a hybrid topology combining the star and ring topologies. This topology is also called a *star-wired ring*. As shown in Figure 10-6, the central device implements the ring by transmitting the signal from device to device in a circular direction.

As with a star topology, devices on a network using the star ring topology are directly connected to a central hub, usually a multi-station access unit (MSAU).

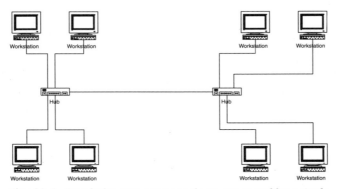

Fig. 10-5. Two hubs, using star topology, connected by a single cable in a bus topology.

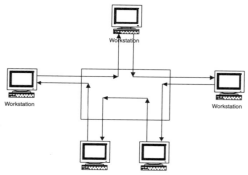

Fig. 10-6. A star ring topology.

As on a ring topology, each device has equal access to the network.

On the star ring topology, if one computer fails, the network will not be affected. Adding or modifying devices does not require the network to be shut down.

For Review

- There are six types of topologies you're expected to know about:

  Bus

  Star

  Ring

  Mesh

  Star Bus

  Star Ring

- A bus topology is a good choice for a temporary network or a small workgroup.

- Cabling costs are higher for a star topology because each device must have a separate cable connecting it to the central hub.

- Ring topologies provide each device with equal access to the network.

- A mesh topology provides for a direct link between each and every device on the network, and quickly becomes impractical as the network grows.

- The initial cost of a star bus topology will be greater than a bus topology; however, the maintenance costs will be less.

- A star ring topology is also known as a star-wired ring topology.

From Here

Chapter 11, "Designing Your Network Architecture," discusses token ring networks, and Ethernet networks are discussed further in Chapter 13, "Network Architectures on the Exam."

CHAPTER 11

Designing Your Network Architecture

Networks are built and launched based on standards that permit limited variation within specific rules and require particular hardware. These rules define and create the architecture of the network. Network architecture describes both the topology and the physical media of the network. By relying on standards, a variety of hardware devices from different vendors can connect to a network without each device requiring a separate interface. Four examples of network architecture are:

- Ethernet
- Token Ring
- AppleTalk
- ARCnet

This chapter provides an overview of Ethernet and Token Ring, with a brief discussion of AppleTalk and ARCnet, and a discussion of network adapter cards. A more detailed look at types of Ethernet architectures can be found in Chapter 13, "Network Architectures on the Exam."

Questions network administrators face when deciding on a network architecture include:

- What applications will be used?
- Where will the applications be located?
- What is the estimated percentage of time for each application's overall use?
- How easy is the initial installation?
- How easy will reconfiguring the network be?
- What are the cost and security concerns?

The answers to these questions help you determine which network architecture is better. The final choice might be a combination of different architectures.

Ethernet

Ethernet is relatively easy and inexpensive to install. Ethernet is a good choice for networks with light-to-moderate workloads consisting of word processing, spreadsheets, electronic mail, and other routine desktop applications.

A disadvantage of Ethernet is the relatively small size of the data frames, which is considered later in this chapter.

Ethernet, a nonproprietary standard based on IEEE 802.3, is currently the most popular network architecture. Ethernet operates with a baseband transmission medium, discussed in the next section. Ethernet networks can be built using twisted-pair, coaxial, and/or fiber-optic cables. Depending on the cabling choice, an Ethernet network can use a bus or star bus topology. IEEE 802.3 defines the transmission speed for Ethernet at either 10 or 100 Mbps.

BASEBAND VERSUS BROADBAND

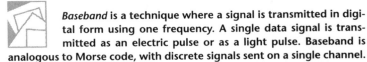 *Baseband* is a technique where a signal is transmitted in digital form using one frequency. A single data signal is transmitted as an electric pulse or as a light pulse. Baseband is analogous to Morse code, with discrete signals sent on a single channel.

Broadband is a technique where a signal is transmitted in analog form using a range of frequencies. Broadband signals, transmitted as electromagnetic or optical waves, are continuous. Broadband is analogous to broadcast cable television with many channels on one cable.

Ethernet uses CSMA/CD (Carrier Sense Multiple Access with Collision Detection) to control media access. This means that each device on the Ethernet network checks the network cable for traffic before sending a data transmission. If CSMA/CD does not detect a transmission already on the cable, it will initiate communication. If a transmission is detected, the device will wait and then retry. If for any reason two devices transmit at the same time, there will be a collision between the two different signals. When this happens, each device will try to send the data again after checking if there is a transmission already on the cable. (For another discussion of the various media access methods see Chapter 12, "Network Topology Building Blocks," next.)

Token Ring

Token Ring is a good choice for larger networks with moderate-to-heavy workloads consisting of transfers of large data files for use in databases or multimedia. A Token Ring operates at 4 or 16 Mbps.

A token ring network, using a star-wired ring topology, is the second most popular network architecture in use today. The usual cabling choices for a token ring network are shielded or unshielded twisted pair, with fiber-optic cable being a more expensive option. At the center of the ring, providing the logical ring topology, is a hub. A hub on a token ring network is also known as a MSAU, multistation access unit, or MAU, media access unit.

A token ring network uses a token-passing method for media access as defined by IEEE 802.5. A token is a signal that moves around the network in sequence from device to device. A device can transmit data only when it has the "free" token. When a device transmits data, the token becomes "busy." As the busy token circulates around the ring, the NIC on each device checks to see if the destination address of the token is meant for that device. After the busy token returns to the sending device, a new token is generated and passed on to the next device. This method of media access allows each device to have equal access to the network.

With the star topology, the failure of one device (unless the device is the MSAU) will not bring the entire network down. A complex process known as *beaconing* automatically helps to isolate problems on a token ring LAN. When a device on a token ring network encounters a serious error, it begins the process to help localize the problem by transmitting a beacon that is a signal sent onto the network. Because all computers in a Token Ring network are responsible for monitoring the network, the computer will continue to send a beacon and the other computers will join the process to help isolate the problem. When the beaconing computer finally receives its own beacon back, it assumes the transmission error has been fixed, and it regenerates a new token so that network communication may resume.

AppleTalk

AppleTalk is a proprietary Apple 230-kbps baseband network. AppleTalk uses the CSMA/CA network media access method. A device using carrier sense multiple access with collision avoidance (CSMA/CA) initiates a signal on the cable to indicate its intent to send before actually sending a data transmission.

AppleTalk networks have a bus topology and are appropriate for smaller networks. AppleTalk can use shielded or unshielded twisted-pair cables and supports up to 32 devices on a network.

ARCnet

Attached Resource Computer network, ARCnet, is an older type of LAN that has proven to be simple, easy to install, and inexpensive. ARCnet uses a token-passing media access method. ARCnet transmission speeds are slow at 2.5 Mbps and can support a maximum of only 255 devices.

An ARCnet advantage is the ability to use various cables (twisted pair, coaxial, and/or fiber optic) on the same network. Traditionally, ARCnet has used a RG-62 A/U coaxial cable with an impedance of 93 ohms.

Network Interface Cards

The network interface card (NIC), also known as a *network adapter card,* controls data transmission between a device and the network cable. A NIC must be installed in each device using the network for the device to communicate with the other devices through the network.

Installing a NIC in a computer's communication bus is similar to installing a video card or a sound card. Frequently, the installer must know the available IRQ (*Interrupt ReQuest*) settings on the device and on the host computer. See Chapter 16, "Taming the Hardware," for more information about IRQs.

Each NIC has a unique address on the computer network. This hardware-level address is commonly called the *MAC address* because NICs operate at the media access control sublayer of the data link layer of the OSI reference model. The MAC sublayer defines the network access method. The MAC address, a 12-digit hexadecimal number, is assigned at the time of manufacture and ordinarily cannot and should not be changed.

Many NICs offer more than one connector. NICs incorporate a transceiver that can interface with one, two, or even three different types of connectors on a single NIC. A transceiver, working at the logical link sublayer of the data link layer of the OSI reference model, performs double duty—as a transmitter and as a receiver. The transmitter part translates the host device's outgoing signals to the type of signal required on the network. For instance, if the network uses coaxial cable, the transceiver will translate the device's outgoing signal into the appropriate electrical signal for that coaxial network. Or, if it is a fiber-optic network, the transmitter component translates the host device's outgoing signal into the light signals used for fiber-optic cable. The receiver part of the transceiver translates the signals taken from the network into signals that can be used by the receiving device.

Popular connector ports on an Ethernet NIC include:

- RJ-45 connector for use with unshielded or shielded twisted-pair Ethernet (10BaseT)

- BNC connector for use with Thin Ethernet (10Base2)

- AUI connector for use with Thick Ethernet (10Base5)

The AUI connector has 15 pins and is occasionally called a *DB15* connector.

The two possible connectors for ports on a Token Ring NIC using unshielded or shielded twisted pair include:

DB-9 Connector (on older networks)

RJ-45 connector

Some NICs used on a 16-Mbps token ring network also include a media filter. A media filter stops noise from UTP cable from being passed onto the network.

ODI and NDIS

Open Data-Link Interface (ODI) is a Novell-Apple specification that standardizes network access methods. It provides a protocol and an API (*Application Programming Interface*) for communicating with network adapter drivers and to support the use of more than one protocol by a single network adapter driver.

Network Device Interface Specification (NDIS) is the Intel-Microsoft specification for network access methods that eliminates the need for manufacturers to write specific drivers for every protocol and NIC combination in the world.

NDIS also allows two or more protocols to be bound to and used by the same NIC. Today, most available NICs support NDIS.

 Both ODI and NDIS 2.x allow multiple protocols to share a single NIC. NDIS 3.0 allows multiple NICs using multiple protocols on a single host. NDIS 3.1 specifies standards for Plug and Play. The exam demands that you know that multiple protocols may be bound to a single NIC.

Data Frames

In operation, the NIC divides the data into small units that are placed within data frames for transmittal to the network cable. Data frame formats are standardized, and the specific format used is dependent on the architecture of the network.

Ethernet Frames

An Ethernet frame can be between 64 and 1518 bytes long. Eighteen bytes are needed for control information. The remaining 46 to 1500 bytes are available for data transmission.

Token Ring Frames

Token Ring frames have beginning and ending delimiters and frames ranging from 4 to 18 kilobytes. Note that these frame sizes are, roughly, at least 3 to 12 times larger than Ethernet frames.

Because of the frame size difference, transferring data from an Ethernet network to a token ring network will proceed at a faster pace than transferring from a token ring network to an Ethernet network. The larger Token Ring frames must be carefully divided into the smaller Ethernet frames. It just takes longer to divide the larger Token Ring data frames into smaller Ethernet frames, than it does to agglomerate many Ethernet frames into a Token Ring frame.

For Review

- The two most popular types of network architecture are:

  Ethernet

  Token Ring

- An Ethernet network uses CSMA/CD for media access control.

- A Token Ring network uses a token passing method for media access control.

- An AppleTalk network uses CSMA/CA for media access control.

- ARCnet uses RG-62 A/U coaxial cable, 93 ohms impedance.

- ODI and NDIS are specifications for network access.

- NDIS and ODI eliminated the need for manufacturers to write a specific driver for every protocol and NIC combination in the world, and they allow multiple protocols to be bound to one NIC.

- Ethernet operates at 10 or 100 Mbps according to IEEE 802.3.

- Token Ring operates both slower (4 Mbps) and faster (16 Mbps) than 10 Mbps Ethernet.

- Ethernet data frames are smaller than Token Ring data frames.

From Here

Ethernet networks are discussed further in Chapter 13, "Network Architectures on the Exam"; IRQs are discussed in Chapter 16, "Taming the Hardware"; and Chapter 12, "Network Topology Building Blocks," discusses media access control mechanisms.

Network Topology Building Blocks

This chapter reviews, enlarges on, and amplifies the discussion of network devices which we began with the Open Systems Interconnect (OSI) reference model in Chapter 9. This time we also rely on, and tangentially review, ideas about popular transmission media that were first presented long ago in Chapter 3, *"Transport Media."*

This chapter defines and explains in greater detail seven important network devices. MCSE candidates must be familiar with the purpose and use of each of these principal networking devices; and, ideally, they should have hands-on experience with most of these devices operating in a network.

Repeaters

Hubs

Bridges

Routers

Brouters

Switches

Gateways

This chapter describes these seven devices to help you apply your knowledge by reviewing some general network structures you can expect to see on the Networking Essentials examination and in real life.

TIP

The devices described in this chapter are changing rapidly in the real world apart from the test environment. The Microsoft exam does not demand that you have all of the latest networking equipment, but rather that you understand the principles that the devices operate by. Because of the rapid evolution of these devices, what is presented here is almost a *stylized* or *traditional* interpretation of the functions of these devices, rather than the endless variety of hybrid equipment actually in use in the worldwide networking environment and available in the current networking marketplace.

Several of these devices are merging functions, and evolving together, as manufacturers compete to create better networks and to find marketing niches that others have not yet exploited. In the real world, it's not uncommon for two or more of these devices to be combined into a single multifunction device, or for a certain subset of functions to be repackaged into a similar device that meets only a special purpose in a particular kind of network configuration.

You will not be expected to know all about the newer hybrid and variant devices for this exam. What you should know is the basic function, purpose, uses, problems, and most common solutions for these fundamental (or archaic) devices.

 Segments.   Before we get too far into the principal network building blocks, we should define the connection between the building blocks—a segment. A network segment is a piece of network transport media (often wire cable) bounded by bridges, brouters, repeaters, routers, or terminators. Electrical signals travel from one computer or network device to another over the transport media of the segment.

Repeaters

A repeater is a basic network device that transmits electrical signals from one segment onto one or more other segments, while restoring the signal waveform and timing. As explained earlier, repeaters can, within limits, keep the network operating when a network grows or when a segment extends beyond the simplest design parameters. Repeaters are typically used to connect LAN cable segments within a building or group of buildings.

Remember from Chapter 9 on the Open Systems Interconnection reference model, that repeaters are used to regenerate and propagate electrical signals because electrical signals weaken (attenuate) as they travel through a network. That's basically what repeaters do—they boost the signal back up to full strength before passing it on, thus allowing the signal to travel further. Here are some additional details, to give you a deeper understanding of how repeaters actually operate in a network.

First, repeaters operate at the physical layer. As shown in Figure 12-1, repeaters physically and electrically connect network segments. Repeaters amplify, reshape, and retime the signal's analog electrical waveform to extend network segment distances. Within very important limits, repeaters extend a *single network*, rather than linking multiple networks together. One limit on the value of repeaters, for example, is that IEEE specifications allow 10Base2 (ThinNet) and 10Base5 (ThickNet) networks to use repeaters to link no more than five segments. These and similar limitations are covered in greater detail later in this chapter.

Repeaters are fairly simple and inexpensive devices, comparatively, and their primary reason for being is not to modify the sig-

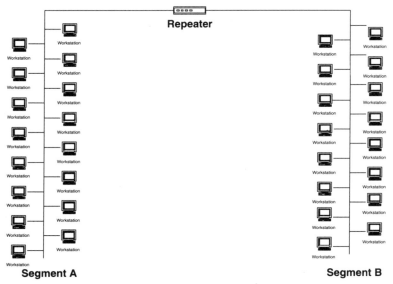

Fig. 12-1. Repeaters link network segments, extending the network.

nal but rather to return the incoming signal to its original state. Unlike an old gossip, repeaters just repeat what they hear, without embellishment or the discretion to leave anything out. So we deduce that, because repeaters don't have the ability to *not* repeat, they contribute to the propagation of broadcast congestion.

 (Jumping ahead, *routers* usually don't pass on broadcast messages—just the opposite of repeaters. More on routers later.)

Considerations with Repeaters

Although repeaters are comparatively inexpensive as LAN devices go, as mentioned, repeaters are also limited in their use. Repeaters don't translate, and they don't make informed decisions about sending messages on. They just blab.

Repeaters don't deal with packet addresses or packet forwarding, so they can't help you reduce network traffic or congestion—as you might guess by now, repeaters contribute to congestion.

Repeaters can only link network segments that use the same media access control scheme. This means repeaters *cannot* connect an Ethernet segment to a Token Ring segment, because they use different media access control methods. Ethernet uses Carrier Sense Multiple Access/Collision Detection (CSMA/CD), and Token Ring uses token passing to control which workstation is allowed to transmit next. This is part of what was previously meant, when we said repeaters extend a single network, rather than linking networks together. Please see the sidebar for more information about access control methods, and particularly the widely popular CSMA/CD access control scheme. Figure 12-2 illustrates the standard CSMA/CD process.

Standard media access control methods provide an orderly process for transmitting data between two computers on the network cable. Standards for the media access control sublayer of the data link layer are defined in Project 802 by the Institute of Electrical and Electronics Engineering.

Here, three methods of media access control are outlined:

1. Carrier Sense Multiple Access with Collision Detection (CSMA/CD)

2. Token passing

3. Demand priority

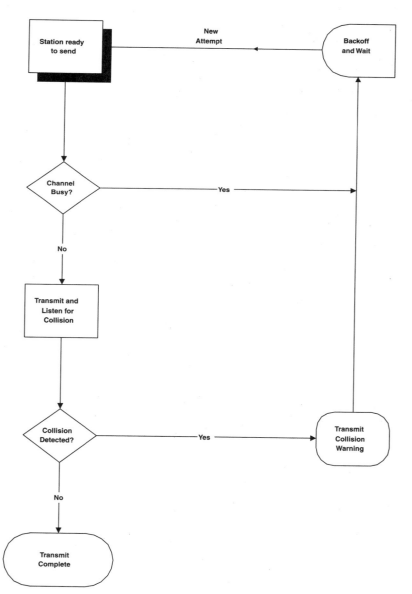

Fig. 12-2. Carrier Sense Multiple Access with Collision Detection (CSMA/CD) resends if a collision is detected.

CSMA/CD

Carrier sense multiple access with collision detection (CSMA/CD) for Ethernet bus networks is defined in IEEE category 802.3. A computer using CSMA/CD checks (some say "listens to") the network cable for traffic before sending a data transmission. If CSMA/CD does not detect a transmission already on the cable (or other transmission media), it initiates communication. If two computers have accidentally begun transmitting at the same time, a "collision" is detected, and each of the computers must wait a random amount of time before reattempting to transmit. The CSMA/CD process just described is shown in Figure 12-2.

A lesser known cousin of CSMA/CD is Carrier Sense Multiple Access with Collision Avoidance (CSMA/CA). CSMA/CA differs from CSMA/CD by initiating a signal on the cable to indicate its *intent* to send data prior to actually sending the data transmission, thereby avoiding collisions. Because collision avoidance is slower, CSMA/CA is not as popular as collision detection. CSMA/CA may also cause significant network traffic problems because it broadcasts its intent to send data. LocalTalk, a kind of Apple network, uses CSMA/CA.

Token Passing

The standards for token passing are given in IEEE 802.4 for token bus networks and IEEE 802.5 for token ring networks. Because IEEE 802.4 is not frequently used, we will discuss only category 802.5 and token ring networks here.

A token is a data frame that is passed in one direction (clockwise) around the token ring. If a computer has the token, that computer has the right to transmit data. Only when it has the token does a computer have the right to transmit. Once the sending computer has received acknowledgment the data have been received by the destination computer, the sending computer generates a new token and forwards the token to the next computer on the ring. If a computer receiving the token has no need to send data, it merely passes the token on to the next computer in the ring.

Although their topology is a ring, token ring networks are typically cabled in a star pattern, with Multistation Access Units (MSAUs) in one or more central wiring closets simulating the logical ring structure.

Demand Priority

IEEE 802.12 provides the standards for the demand priority access method. In demand priority, the hub controls which computer has permission to transmit data. The hub polls each computer in a predetermined order. If a computer wants access to the cable, the computer sends a data frame to the hub when polled. From the data frames received from a polling cycle, the hub determines which data frames are high priority and, therefore, must be processed first, and which are normal priority.

Collision Domain

An Ethernet collision domain is the network area within which frames that have collided were propagated. As this chapter progresses you'll see that repeaters and hubs enlarge the collision domain and proliferate collisions; however, bridges, routers, and LAN switches do not enlarge collision domains, which makes for happier network administrators.

Repeaters also introduce propagation delay into networks. A small but measurable amount of time is required for a repeater to do its job of regenerating, retiming, and propagating the signal. With multiple repeaters on a network, propagation delays can add up and negatively influence network performance. While we're talking about network delays, it's time to mention another term, *latency,* used to describe the time network devices need to do their jobs.

Latency

A device's *latency* is the time between receiving a signal and sending the signal back out again. As you might expect, short latencies are, in general, better than long latencies. The more complicated the network device, and the more complex its function, the longer the latency a device will impose on signals passing through it.

Remember, repeaters work at the lowest, *physical* layer of the OSI reference model. They provide physical continuity to the transport medium, by physically linking one network segment to the next, while also electronically linking the two segments by regenerating and amplifying the data signal across the same physical link.

Repeaters may also be used to join different types of physical transport media *if the differing media* use the same protocol(s), the same media access scheme, and the same transmission technique. Media conversion devices can also be used in conjunction with repeaters. Media conversion devices are available to link coaxial cable segments to UTP or fiber-optic cable segments, to link 100 Mbps Ethernet UTP to 100 Mbps Ethernet fiber-optic cable, etc.

There are many technical restrictions on how Ethernet cabling can be installed. Some are distance limitations related to the type of cable (or transport medium) that is used. Others are technical restrictions on the maximum number of repeaters and cable segments between any two stations on the network. These restrictions are so commonly used and important that you should expect to memorize them. The most important Ethernet cabling rules are summarized in Tables 12-1 and 12-2.

The Ethernet "5-4-3 Rule"

The Ethernet "5-4-3 rule" for connecting segments says that up to 5 trunk segments can be connected, with 4 repeaters, if no more than 3 segments contain workstations (on coaxial cable). Five segments, four repeaters, three populated segments. So, any possible path between any two workstations (or network devices) on an unbridged/unrouted network may not pass through more than 4 repeaters or hubs, nor more than 3 populated cable segments. Table 12-2 shows the maximum network size limits that the IEEE standards and the 5-4-3 rule impose on the ThickNet and ThinNet Ethernet networks.

As you can guess from the last paragraph, bridges and routers are used by experts to push networks beyond the standard limits shown in Tables 12-1 and 12-2.

Because 10BaseT is a point-to-point network medium usually wired in a star pattern, you can probably remember it best by recalling one end of the cable typically beginning at a repeater or hub, and the other end of the cable connecting at a computer or other network device. For the exam, you'll need to know that 10Base2 and 10BaseT both can handle up to 1023 stations on a single network without bridging or routing, according to specifications.

Hubs

A *hub* is a multiport device that allows several cables (or, more generally, several sections of a particular transport medium) to attach. In a star topology network like 10BaseT, a *hub* plays the central role, bringing all the cable runs together into one device, as in Figure 12-3.

Hubs generally redistribute incoming signals to all ports simultaneously. Active hubs contain electronics similar to repeaters to regenerate and retime the signal between each hub port. Passive

Table 12-1. Standards Required by Popular 10-Mbps Networking Architectures.

				10-Mbps IEEE Standards			
Basename	Nickname	Cabling	Typical topology	Typical bandwidth	Maximum unrepeated segment length	Maximum device nodes per unrepeated segment	Minimum node spacing	Maximum network trunk length
10BaseT	UTP Ethernet	UTP, category 3, 4, or 5	star	10 Mbps	100 meters or 11.5-decibel maximum loss	1023 per network	star topology, 2.5 meters, 8.2 feet	does not apply to star topology
10Base2	Thin Ethernet, Coax ThinNet, CheaperNet	50 ohm; RG-58 A/U	local bus	10 Mbps	185 meters or 606 feet	30 per trunk, 1023 per network	0.5 meters or 20 inches	925 meters or 3035 feet, with 5 segments and 4 repeaters
10Base5	ThickNet	50 ohm; RG-8, RG-11	bus	10 Mbps	500 meters or 1,640 feet	100	2.5 meters or 8.2 feet	8200 feet, with 5 segments and 4 repeaters
10BaseF	fiber Ethernet	Optical fiber	point-to-point	10 Mbps	to 2,000 meters, depending	varies	varies	does not apply to point-to-point transport

Table 12-2. The Ethernet "5-4-3 Rule": 5 Segments Connected by 4 Repeaters Can Have Only 3 Segments with Workstations.

	Maximum segments	Maximum repeaters	Maximum populated segments	Maximum workstations per segment	Maximum workstations per network	Maximum segment length	Maximum network distance
			The Ethernet "5-4-3 rule"				
10Base2 Coax ThinNet	5	4	3	30	90	185 meters	925 meters
10Base5 ThickNet	5	4	3	100	300	500 meters	2500 meters

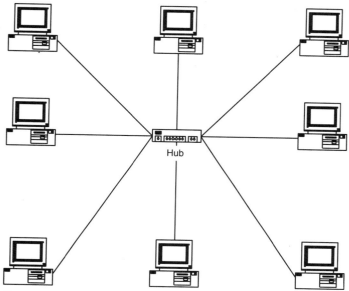

Fig. 12-3. Hubs are the center of the star topology.

hubs are primarily signal splitters, similar in function to the cable-TV splitters one might use on a home coaxial TV cable antenna. Either way, hubs propagate network congestion, along with repeaters.

10BaseT WITH NO HUB
There is at least one way to use 10BaseT Ethernet to connect two computers without a hub: A special "cross-over" or "flipped" cable can run between the two 10BaseT ports. A two-node Ethernet network is produced, even without a hub!

Hubs are sometimes referred to as *concentrators* or as *multiport* repeaters.

For Review

- Hubs and repeaters contribute to network broadcast congestion.

- Hubs and repeaters don't filter, they retransmit all data in all directions.

Table 12-3. Hubs Operate at the Physical Layer of the Open Systems Interconnection (OSI) Reference Model.

Layer	Network Devices Operating at This OSI Level
Application	gateways
Presentation	
Session	
Transport	
Network	routers, brouters
Data link	bridges, brouters
Physical	hubs, network interface cards (NICs), repeaters

■ In Table 12-3, hubs have been added to the list of devices we first presented in Chapter 9 on the OSI reference model.

Bridges

Bridges are smarter than repeaters, but not as smart as routers or switches. Because they are self-learning, bridges are easy to administer. In this chapter, bridges are the first devices we'll cover that forward data traffic toward its specific destination—later we'll discuss three more forwarding devices: brouters, routers, and switches.

Bridges connect two or more LANs, and they make informed decisions about forwarding incoming signals. A bridge looks at the destination and source addresses of each frame, and either drops the frame, transmits the frame across the bridge to the other LAN, or broadcasts the frame in all directions.

So, bridges can isolate exclusively local traffic, keeping local frames from entering neighboring LANs. This is how bridges are often used—to separate high-traffic areas such as busy local work-groups on a LAN. Bridges are relatively inexpensive, uncomplicated to use, and easy to administer in achieving their isolation task.

Most bridges connect two LANs. However, some bridges do connect three or more LANs, so in the remainder of this section you'll find occasional mentions of bridges with more than two "sides." Do not be alarmed—these bridges have three or more ports, one connected to each LAN.

A bridge works at the data link level of a network (at the media access sublayer), copying a data frame from one side of the bridge to the other along the communications path. In a way, LAN segments connected by a bridge form a single, larger, logical or *bridged* network. In fact, bridges usually connect two *similar* kinds of networks, such as two Ethernet networks or two Token Ring networks so that users on either network can access resources on the other.

Regular bridges are unable to translate protocols, so they cannot be used to link LANs using different network protocols. Bridges connect similar networks because they must—bridges can only connect networks with the same media access scheme, so that a regular bridge would not, for instance, connect a token ring network with an Ethernet network.

Source Route Bridges

The IEEE defines two main types of bridges. Source route bridging (SRB) is used between Token Ring networks and is documented in IEEE 802.5. Token Ring networks use source route bridging, where client computers find paths to destinations, and include the route path inside each data frame. Just like all other network devices on a Token Ring network, bridges have to wait their turn to receive the token before they forward data. Source route bridges are often the only option available for bridging Token Ring networks.

Transparent Bridges

The other main type of bridge, a transparent bridge, is defined in IEEE 802.1. Transparent bridges learn, and they keep local traffic local. Bridges are *transparent* to other devices on an Ethernet network, in that other devices don't need to be told there is a bridge present. Most networks do not require configuration changes to become bridged networks.

A bridge's primary function is to connect distinct network segments (usually referring to a physical length of wire) and carefully forward traffic between them, isolating them from unnecessary cross traffic at the same time. And bridges can also allow you to extend the maximum size of the network by exceeding the maximum segment length, attached device count, and/or number of repeaters for a network. This is a powerful motivator if a large, smoothly functioning network is already built and *only* needs a minor extension beyond the technical limits.

Another advantage of bridges is that they can easily allow you to connect two LANs that have different physical transport media. If one LAN uses 10BaseT unshielded twisted pair (UTP) and the other uses 10Base2 coaxial cable, for instance, and the LANs otherwise use the same media access scheme and protocols, a bridge can quickly connect the two networks.

Transparent "Learning" Bridges

A learning bridge monitors the MAC (Open Systems Interconnection reference model data link layer, media access control sublayer) addresses on both (or all) sides of the bridge. They listen and monitor the source MAC address of every frame on the network. A learning bridge attempts to learn which MAC addresses are on (coming from) which side by matching and recording the source computer's MAC address with the physical bridge interface (or port) that frame was received on. Knowing which physical interface on the bridge leads to the source computer for each frame on the network allows the bridge to build its bridging table.

TIP
When a bridge is mentioned on the exam, it's most likely that the bridge is a **transparent learning bridge**, because this kind of bridge is the most commonly found in the real networking world.

Bridges want to learn which addresses are on which network segment to develop their bridging table so that later messages can be forwarded to the correct network segment. Learning bridges reduce traffic on the network by *not forwarding* frames to the other side(s) of the bridge if the frames are targeted for MAC addresses on *the same* side of the bridge.

By knowing which "source" computers are on which side(s) of the bridge, a bridge can tell where to forward frames as they come in, or not to forward them at all, if the source and destination computers are on the same side. Bridges simply drop frames "into the bit bucket" if the source and destination addresses are both on the same side of the bridge. This is good for networks because it isolates local high-traffic areas and reduces unnecessary broadcast traffic. A repeater in the same location would aggravate network congestion, so bridges, with their additional intelligence, can solve problems that repeaters can't.

Eventually, bridges automatically build nearly comprehensive local MAC address and port tables for frame forwarding. After a bridge has its MAC address forwarding table built, it can efficiently decide, whenever it receives a frame, whether the frame should cross the bridge or not. Bridges usually have only one designated pathway to a particular MAC address. On the other hand, routers, which are discussed in the next section, can use several paths to a node.

We've covered what bridges do if the destination address is on the same side, or the other side(s) of the bridge. What about frames with unfamiliar, foreign destination addresses?

Bridges Broadcast Unknown Frames

When a bridge receives a frame destined for an address that it doesn't recognize from the bridging table, by default that frame is forwarded across the bridge to the other network(s). This unlearned default behavior sometimes gets bridges a bad reputation—you can see how this default can cause bridges to possibly propagate broadcast storms and can otherwise contribute to increased broadcast overhead and congestion.

Bridges also forward all incoming traffic that is identified as broadcast traffic. If every computer on the segment is meant to receive a message, bridges dutifully pass the message on to everyone.

Bridging Considerations

First, bridges are being replaced by switches and routers, because, as switches and routers come down in cost, they can provide many of the same services and more, at little additional cost.

Nonroutable protocols, such as NetBEUI (*NetBIOS Extended User Interface*) and DLC (*Data Link Control*) can cross bridges—sometimes these protocols are even referred to as *bridged* protocols.

Bridges are slower than repeaters. It takes bridges longer because they have to check the MAC address of each frame before deciding what to do with it, even to drop it. Routers can be even slower than bridges when they are configured to act as bridges, because routers don't always have all the same hardware components that bridges have.

Bridges contribute the most on networks with several servers, each with affiliate clients, and most user activity is confined on a small number of dedicated servers. This creates finite areas of traffic that can be isolated from each other with bridges.

In networks that are stable and unchanging, bridges can help control congestion without contributing seriously to broadcast storms. However, whenever a bridged network is reconfigured, the bridging tables might need to be rebuilt from scratch. While the bridging tables are being reconstructed a broadcast storm is inevitable. Remember, bridging relies heavily on broadcasting. By default, bridges broadcast frames bound for unknown MAC addresses.

Real-World Bridged Networking

The following brief comments about bridges in the real world are meant to round out your knowledge of bridges.

Aka Relays

In some literature, and in some networking environments, bridges are called *MAC layer relays, layer two relays,* or even *data link layer relays.* This terminology refers to a bridge's ability to forward data frames in the "correct" direction between networks, based on data from one layer of the OSI reference model. In the next section you'll see that routers are sometimes also referred to as *relays*—routers are network layer or layer three relays.

Remote Bridges

Remote bridges come in pairs. Each remote bridge has an Ethernet interface on one side and a serial interface on the other. The serial link runs between the two bridges. If a wide area network (WAN) requires a connection in a location where installing network cables is infeasible or impractical, a remote bridge sometimes can fill the bill. A high-speed modem and telephone line (or other telecommunication link) can be used over the serial link between the two remote bridges.

Other Bridges

As mentioned at the beginning of this chapter, most network devices are evolving to embrace more and more features specific to the needs of particular networks. Bridges are no exception. For instance, some bridges incorporate error correction services to reduce that load on workstations. More expensive **translating bridges** actually can connect Ethernet and Token Ring networks, allowing computers on both sides to communicate across the bridge even though they have differing media access schemes. Also, many powerful bridges are able to connect network segments operating at different speeds, 10 and 100 Mbps, for instance. These are **speed buffering bridges** that connect LAN segments with similar architectures but different transmission speeds.

For Review

- Bridges filter, forward, or flood incoming frames based on the MAC address destination of the frame.

- Bridging is most commonly used to separate high-traffic areas on a LAN.

- Transparent bridging is used in Ethernet environments and relies on bridging tables built from real network traffic.

- If the sending and receiving addresses are located on the same side of the bridge, a bridge will reduce network traffic by *not forwarding* the data across the bridge.

- Bridges work at the data link layer of the OSI reference model, at the media access control sublayer.

- Bridges are a quick, transparent fix because they work without any reconfiguration of or interaction with the other devices on the network, and without changes in protocols, addressing, or frame formats.

- A bridge can join networks with different physical transport media.

- Bridges can create broadcast storms by forwarding the data to all nodes, if the bridge does not already know the destination MAC address of the incoming data.

Routers

Routers work at the network, or third, layer of the OSI reference model. The router uses network layer information to choose the best path or *route* a packet will take as it moves from the sending computer to the receiving computer, or to decide to ignore or drop the packet. Routers can also be forced, with a manually entered *static* route, to send packets for a certain node by any pathway that the network administrator desires.

Routers can improve network performance because a router can select, and in many cases learn and remember, the best route for data to take in reaching a specific network address. Routers can curtail or even eliminate broadcast storms because, by default, routers do not forward broadcasts.

Another big advantage that routers have is that they can connect dissimilar networks, like Ethernet, Token Ring, X.25, Frame Relay, and FDDI. Routers can also be a network's primary connection to the Internet. Routing onto the Internet calls for additional security concerns which can be studied at this URL:

http://www.microsoft.com/security/

Although routers have traditionally been powerful hardware devices of their own, there are ways routing can be done by adding software to a computer connected to two or more networks, so that the computer meets the basic definition of a router. Computers permanently connected to more than one network are referred to as *multihomed*. Multihomed computers have more than one network adapter card. For additional details on the Microsoft view of routing, please see the "TCP/IP Routing Basics for Windows NT," article in the Microsoft Knowledge Base: Article-ID: Q140859.

Routers can do everything that bridges do, only better. Routers can segment networks, they can connect network segments using different transport media, and they can filter local traffic and forward outbound traffic in the "correct" direction. Even better than bridges, routers collect and share routing information so that they can choose the best path for sending outbound data to its destination.

Routers are often the network device of choice on large networks, in contrast to bridges. Although routers are generally slower than bridges, bridges are at an increasing disadvantage as networks become larger, because bridges forward broadcasts and also because in large networks there can be many redundant paths between two nodes—bridges abhor redundant paths.

Routers use routing protocols to share information among neighboring routers, so that together they can find routes to bypass or lessen the load on slow or broken connections.

Routing Metrics
Routers use one or more metrics to choose the best path to forward network traffic to its destination. Some routing protocols choose the best path by *hop count*, minimizing the number of routers between the source and the destination; other routing protocols choose the best path by checking available bandwidth

and calculating a route that provides the optimal service at that time. Every router maintains or creates tables of available routes (and usually the associated metric or cost of each route) and uses various cost algorithms to choose the best route.

The router first figures out whether a packet's destination is on a local network or a remote network. To allow communication with a node on another network, the router then creates a packet that contains the data "payload," the sender's address (the source address), and the destination node's address (the target address). Because the destination address is on a remote network, the data packet is prepared and, if necessary, sent to a router (or gateway) attached to the local network.

Before being sent on their way, the data are prepared by being put inside (encapsulated in) the appropriate frame for transmission across the first intervening network toward the destination network. As part of their everyday job, routers remove and replace these outer encapsulation frames all the time, so they are used to dealing with frames and are good at removing and replacing them.

A packet may travel through many network routers before arriving at its destination. When a router along the way receives a data packet, it looks inside the frame encapsulating the packet and checks to find the target network—the network *containing* the destination node address. The router then consults its routing table and chooses the best path to the target network, then encapsulates the packet as appropriate for the next intervening network, and passes the packet along its way. Each router between the source network and destination network does these same operations, in turn.

In its travels, none of the intervening routers ever bother to look at its destination **node** address—all along the way the routers concentrate only on getting the packet to the right *network*. That is, none of the routers look at the destination node address until the packet gets to the network that contains the target node.

When a packet reaches a router on the packet's target or destination network, that router recognizes the packet as being destined for a directly connected network. The final router then checks the packet's destination node number in an address mapping table that connects device MAC addresses to network layer node addresses. Once the router finds the correct node address, it sends the packet directly to the MAC address for the destination node.

Deciding Between a Router and a Bridge

Routers are slower and more costly than bridges. They're slower because it takes additional time to look inside the packets, find the addresses, and choose an optimal route for each packet. And routers are smarter and more versatile than bridges, so you may gain more for a router's higher price. You'll certainly receive more functionality from a router than a bridge, because most routers can also function as bridges, in a pinch.

Installing a router may do you little good if your network requires heavy use of nonroutable protocols (NetBEUI, DEC LAT, etc.). However, never fear, sometimes this limitation can be surmounted by encapsulation of the unroutable protocol inside a routable protocol, but that level of network magic is beyond the scope of this book, or this exam, for that matter. Table 12-4 lists routable and nonroutable protocols.

Routers were once called *gateways*. This is especially true in the Internet community. The term *gateway*, which is discussed later in this chapter after brouters and switches, now has many meanings. Fortunately, the Microsoft exam focuses on only one primary meaning of the word.

Another term used for a router is *layer three relay*, referring to the network layer of the OSI reference model as layer three.

Table 12-4.
Routable and Nonroutable Protocols.*

Routable Protocols	Nonroutable Protocols
AppleTalk (DDP)	DEC LAT
DECnet	DLC
IP	NetBEUI
IPX	
OSI	
XNS	

* Some protocols are routable, and some aren't. NetBEUI, DLC, and LAT are the most likely nonroutable protocols to show up on the exam.

Classless Interdomain Routing (CIDR)

CIDR is a newer routing technique, not yet on this Microsoft exam, based on route aggregation. CIDR allows routers to group routes together to reduce the size of the routing tables, particularly the massive routing tables used near the Internet backbone. CIDR allows several or many networks to appear as a single larger entity, and CIDR relies on routers nearer to the aggregated networks to provide detailed, specific routes once traffic has become local to its destination.

For Review

- Routers filter and forward packets based on network layer information.

- By default, routers don't forward broadcasts.

- Routers can do everything bridges can do, and more.

- Routers can introduce delays and latency because they have more work to do.

- Routers talk to each other, using routing protocols, to share routes and metrics.

- Routers choose the best path to route each packet.

Brouters

Brouters combine components of a bridge and a router. While some transport protocols (for example, TCP/IP or IPX) use the brouter as a router, other nonroutable protocols use the brouter as a bridge.

For example, although the NetBEUI protocol is not routable, NetBEUI can cross a bridge *or a brouter* to another part of the bridged network. On the other hand, routable protocols use a brouter as a router. So, brouters can do routing for data forwarding, and bridging, both in the same device. Table 12-5 includes brouters in the OSI reference model at the network and data link layers.

A bridge usually offers only one path to a connected network. A router may offer several paths to individual destinations on neighboring networks.

A brouter handles nonroutable data frames, NetBEUI frames, for example, just the same as a bridge would in the same position. If the source and destination addresses are both on the same

Table 12-5. Open Systems Interconnection (OSI) Reference Model.*

Layer	Network Devices Operating at This OSI Level
Application	gateways
Presentation	
Session	
Transport	
Network	routers, brouters
Data Link	bridges, brouters
Physical	repeaters, network interface cards (NICs)

* Brouters work at both the data link (MAC) layer and the network layer, depending on the protocol.

"side" of the brouter, a brouter will drop the local frames rather than forwarding them.

Brouters can be a convenient multiprotocol networking solution because they combine all data forwarding services into a single device that examines all incoming data, regardless of protocol, and forwards it appropriately.

Switches

Switches are multiport devices that create temporary paths to send frames directly to a device based on its MAC address.

Switches use temporary connections to route traffic over the network. Switches typically use the data link layer, media access control (MAC) sublayer, for addressing. The switch hardware internally forwards each frame to the correct output port. In contrast, routers use software programs to choose and route frames. So, switches improve performance by using hardware, which is faster, rather than software to forward frames to the proper node.

In a routed network, computers must wait until "the line is free" to communicate, because only one communication can take place at a time. In a switched network, a dedicated physical circuit path (a "connection") exists between sender and receiver for the duration of the "call," and other paths remain available for other computers to use, at the same time.

Bridges and switches both filter based on MAC layer addresses. By segmenting the LAN at the MAC level, bridges and switches can both allow network designers to extend the maximum size of the network. Like bridges, switches allow designers to exceed the standard maximum segment length, attached device count, and/or number of repeaters for a network. Switches can be helpful if a large, smoothly functioning network is already built and needs only a minor extension beyond the technical limits.

Gateways

Gateways generally work at the top, application layer of the OSI reference model. Gateways are sophisticated, slow, and often powerful devices and software programs that translate protocols, architecture, data formats, etc., between dissimilar networks or dissimilar environments. A gateway is usually also housed on a dedicated computer that performs one specific interpretation and translation task for the whole network.

Some gateways can access and use all seven layers of the OSI reference model, so it is not enough to simply say that "gateways work at the application layer." Gateways are for specific purposes, and they are usually unique and expensive. Because they're usually designed for a focused and limited purpose, it's easy to over-generalize about gateways.

Perhaps the best way to explain gateways would be to give some examples. One typical example is that a gateway can perform the role of an e-mail translator. Incoming e-mail in several formats can be converted to a single format for all local users (if all local users have a single e-mail format) for instance. When e-mail is sent back out through the gateway, it might uniformly convert the e-mail back to another format for external delivery.

Another common solution provided by a gateway is to connect a Novell server to a Microsoft network, without installing Novell client software on every Microsoft client computer. A special-purpose gateway can be installed that handles all format and protocol translation back and forth for both the Microsoft clients and the Novell server.

Generally, gateways provide specific translation duties for a network. The entity on the other side of the gateway can be some-

Table 12-6. Open Systems Interconnection (OSI) Reference Model.

Layer	Network Devices Operating at This OSI Level
Application	gateways
Presentation	
Session	
Transport	
Network	routers, brouters
Data Link	bridges, brouters, switches
Physical	hubs, repeaters, network interface cards (NICs), switches

* Various gateways operate at all levels of the Open Systems Interconnection (OSI) model—most commonly gateways work at the application level.

thing other than a LAN of personal computers, for example, it could be a bulletin-board service or a mainframe computer.

A mainframe gateway is another typical example. A gateway often exists between an IBM mainframe and a LAN of Microsoft client computers. IBM mainframes typically expect to deal only with dumb terminals, rather than sophisticated client computers—a gateway between them can translate the IBM mainframe's SNA network protocol for the PCs, and also translate the PCs' output to make them appear as dumb terminals for the mainframe's convenience. Table 12-6 shows gateways at the top level of the OSI reference model.

For Review

- Gateways can convert protocols, formats, and system architectures.
- Gateways connect networks to dissimilar networks and dissimilar environments.
- Gateways provide two-way translation services.
- Gateways convert data so that applications can work transparently across the network.

For Further Information

Here are some Web sites that contain useful information about devices discussed in this chapter. These are manufacturers, and as such, their marketing and sales emphasis must be tempered with a grain of salt. Nonetheless, there are excellent sources of information available in white papers and even marketing pages on these sites—and in the world of networking, MCSEs will be expected to be aware of these resources.

3Com White Papers

`http://www.3com.com/technology/tech_net/white_papers/index.html`

Bay Networks Study Overview

`http://support.baynetworks.com/training/study.html`

Cisco White Papers

`http://www.cisco.com/warp/public/779/servpro/news/white.htm`

Ascend Resource Library

`http://www.ascend.com/169.html`

CHAPTER 13

Network Architectures on the Exam

This chapter focuses on the variations of Ethernet architecture and provides brief discussions of Token Ring and ARCnet network architectures.

Ethernet

Ethernet can be found in every sort of LAN environment. Using a bus or star bus topology, Ethernet baseband networks transmit data over twisted-pair, coaxial, and fiber-optic cables at a rate of 10 or 100 Mbps. The Ethernet specifications are defined by IEEE 802.3, with carrier sense multiple access with collision detection (CSMA/CD). See Chapter 11, "Designing Your Network Architecture," for more information on media access control mechanisms.

There are several variations of Ethernet shown in Table 13-1. Each variation uses a different type of cable and has specific workstation/distance limitations. Originally, Ethernet was designed using thick coaxial cable (10Base5). The second variation of Ethernet uses thin coaxial cable (10Base2). While both types of coaxial cable provide adequate performance, they use a bus topology that makes reconfiguring a network more difficult. The third variation of Ethernet, using twisted-pair cables (10BaseT), is currently the most popular due to its star topology, ease of installation, rea-

Table 13-1. Ethernet Uses Baseband Transmissions at 10 Mbps.

Ethernet Variations Defined by IEEE 802.3:

10BaseT	twisted pair
10Base2	ThinNet
10Base5	ThickNet
10BaseF	fiber optic

sonable cost, and the option of using existing wiring schemes. A fourth variation mentioned briefly in this chapter is 10BaseF—Ethernet over fiber-optic cable.

10BaseT—Twisted-Pair Ethernet

10BaseT uses unshielded twisted-pair cabling and is frequently referred to as UTP Ethernet or twisted-pair Ethernet. As defined by IEEE, the term 10BaseT refers to a 10-Mbps transmission rate over a baseband medium using unshielded twisted-pair cable.

10BaseT has a maximum cable length of 100 meters (328 feet) from the NIC to the hub. This means that workstations cannot be placed at a distance greater than 328 feet from the wiring closet. And a minimum cable length of 2.5 meters (8 feet) is required between the hub and the workstation.

Devices are organized with hubs in a layout resembling a star pattern while internally using a bus signaling system. The number of devices connected to a hub depends on the number of ports on the hub, usually between 4 and 24 ports. The hub also commonly functions as a repeater. A maximum of 1024 devices can be placed on a 10BaseT network.

UTP cable uses RJ-45 connectors. RJ-45 connectors, although similar to the RJ-11 connectors used with telephone jacks, have eight wire conductors, twice the number of conductors on a RJ-11.

10BaseT installations require twisted-pair cable with a category 3, 4, or 5 rating. Category 3 is adequate to transmit data up to 10 Mbps. Category 4 has a maximum transmission speed of 16 Mbps. Category 5 supports data transfer rates up to 100 Mbps. By using category 5 twisted-pair cable during a new 10BaseT installation now, increasing network bandwidth later becomes more straightforward. See Chapter 3, "Transport Media," for a discussion of the different categories of twisted-pair cables.

SHIELDED TWISTED PAIR

Shielded twisted pair (STP), although used less frequently, has two advantages over UTP. First, STP is less susceptible to electrical interference and crosstalk. STP can also support a higher transmission rate for a greater distance. STP is seldom used because the cable is more expensive, less flexible than UTP, and harder to install.

10BaseT networks are the easiest to install and maintain, compared to 10Base2 and 10Base5. Twisted pair is also lighter, less expensive, and more flexible than ThinNet or ThickNet. Installation is often as easy as plugging the cable connector into a jack, similar to modern telephone hookups. Because each device on a 10BaseT network has a direct cable connection to a central hub, the failure of one device (other than the hub) does not bring the network down. And adding or removing a device does not require the network to be shut down. 10BaseT networks are easily expanded.

100BASEX (AKA FAST ETHERNET)

Most Ethernet networks currently operate at 10 Mbps. As more bandwidth is required, there will be a migration to the 100 Mbps offered by Fast Ethernet. Many network devices, including NICs and hubs, are now available in a 10/100 version that will accommodate both speeds.

By installing category 5 twisted-pair cables today, with the ability to eventually transmit at 100 Mbps in a new installation, you actually save money preparing for an upcoming migration.

The IEEE's 100BaseX specification, Fast Ethernet, uses the same media access mechanism (CSMA/CD) as other Ethernet networks— at the faster 100-Mbps transmission speed.

10Base2—ThinNet

10Base2 is also known as *ThinNet, thin wire Ethernet, thin Ethernet,* or *thin coax.* The term 10Base2 is derived from 10 Mbps over a baseband medium and the ability to carry a signal approximately 2 × 100 meters, although the actual maximum distance is 185 meters.

ThinNet supports up to 30 devices, in a bus topology, per cable segment. Devices include repeaters and workstations. Up to five cable segments can be joined together with repeaters. However, a maximum of 90 devices can be supported on this network.

ThinNet, unlike ThickNet described in the following, does not use drop cables. Each computer is directly connected to the Thin-Net cable by a BNC T-connector (see sidebar) attached to the computer's NIC. ThinNet uses the internal *transceiver on the NIC* to receive and transmit signals.

A minimum distance of 0.5 meters (20 inches) is required on the ThinNet cable between each device.

 ThinNet can carry a signal up to 185 meters (607 feet). ThinNet transmits data at 10 Mbps.

ThinNet requires RG-58 A/U or RG-58 C/U, the military specification for the same cable.

NOTE
Remember that even though RG-58 C/U coaxial cable, for use with cable television signals, is less expensive than RG-58 A/U, it is not appropriate to use RG-58 C/U on a 10Base2 network.

RG-58 A/U coaxial cable is about ¼ inch wide, and is flexible (compared to ThickNet) and supports transmission speeds up to 10 Mbps.

Each end of the ThinNet cable must be terminated, using 50-ohm terminators, and one end of the cable must be grounded for the signal to be transmitted properly. (See sidebar for information on terminating and grounding.) Terminators are also referred to as *terminating resistors.*

ThinNet can be used for a greater distance than 10BaseT and provides greater security. ThinNet is easier to install than Thick-Net because ThinNet is more flexible and is easier to connect to the network adapter card. Configuration and installation are relatively easy with each device connecting directly to the network cable using the BNC T-connector attached to the NIC. 10Base2 cable is also less expensive than 10Base5.

With its bus topology, adding or reconfiguring devices on a 10Base2 network requires the network to be shut down. If a single device fails, the network will often fail as well.

A 10Base2 network is most appropriate for a small, stable network that will not require many changes or expansion.

BNC CONNECTORS

The exact source of the acronym *BNC* has been lost. Possible phrases are British Naval Connector, British National Connector, Bayonet Nut Connector, and Bayonet Neill Concelman. BNC is shorter.

There are actually three types of BNC connectors.

1. The basic BNC connector is the male component and is located at the end of each cable.

2. A BNC T-connector is the female component, connecting two cables to a NIC.

3. A BNC barrel connector connects two cables together directly.

TERMINATING VERSUS GROUNDING

A 10Base2 or a 10Base5 network must be terminated at both ends of the bus. A terminator placed on each end of the coaxial cable prevents the electrical signals from bouncing back onto the network. The terminator resistance must exactly match the cable being used. A RG-58 A/U coaxial cable requires a 50-ohm terminating resistor. As an example, a 93-ohm terminating resistor from an ARCnet network with RG-62 A/U cable will not work properly on a 10Base2 or 10Base5 network.

 A 10Base2 or a 10Base5 network should be *grounded* at only one end to prevent ground loops. More than one ground on the network will cause errors and can also damage equipment.

THE 5-4-3 RULE

The 5-4-3 rule refers to Ethernet networks using coaxial cabling. Five segments can be connected, using four repeaters, and only three of the segments can have devices attached. See Table 12-2 to review the requirements.

10Base5—ThickNet

One of the topologies defined by IEEE 802.3 is 10Base5. 10Base5 is also referred to as ThickNet or "standard" Ethernet. The term *10Base5* is derived from transmission speeds of 10 Mbps, a baseband medium, and a maximum segment length of 500 meters.

A typical use of 10Base5 (ThickNet) is as the backbone to connect smaller ThinNet networks within a building. ThickNet costs more than ThinNet and can transmit data for a greater distance (500 meters or 1640 feet). ThickNet transmits data at 10 Mbps.

10Base5 coaxial cabling is about ½ inch thick and is quite rigid and difficult to work with.

ThickNet can support up to 100 nodes per cable segment. Up to five cable segments of ThickNet can be connected using repeaters. The entire length of the connected cable from end to end cannot exceed 2500 meters (8200 feet).

ThickNet connects each node or LAN with a drop cable (also known as *transceiver cable*). Bridges and routers, in addition to workstations, all count when applying the maximum devices rules. The drop cables are connected to external transceivers that are then connected to the network adapter card on a workstation. Shielded-pair cable is usually used for the drop cables. Drop cables can be 50 meters (164 feet) in length. The network adapters use 15-pin AUI (Attachment Unit Interface) connectors. These connectors are occasionally referred to as *DB-15*. The external transceiver is attached to the DB-15 connector. Figure 13-1 shows ThickNet connecting to transceivers, ThinNet drop cables, and workstations.

In some cases a network adapter card can interface with internal or external transceivers, so a transceiver setting or jumper must be set to configure a workstation.

A minimum distance of 2.5 meters (8 feet) is required on the ThickNet cable between each connection.

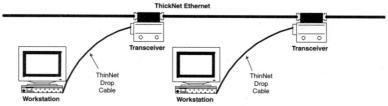

Fig. 13-1. ThickNet uses external transceivers and drop cables.

As with ThinNet, each end of the cable segment must be terminated, using 50-ohm terminators, for signals to be properly transmitted on the network.

10Base5 cable costs more than 10Base2, and can be used over a greater distance. 10Base5, like 10Base2, uses a bus topology, so that reconfiguring the network after the initial installation can be difficult. And, if a failure occurs anywhere on the network, the operation of the network is likely to be influenced.

10BaseF—Fiber Optic

10BaseF is derived from transmission speeds of up to 10 Mbps, over a baseband medium, using fiber-optic cable. Data signals are transmitted using pulses of light. A 10BaseF network uses a star topology, and each device directly connects to a central hub. It is often used as a "backbone," or to connect buildings on a campus.

Fiber-optic cable, a run of which can extend for up to 2000 meters (6562 feet), provides more security than twisted-pair or coaxial cable because, today, only the most wealthy can afford the knowledge and equipment necessary to surreptitiously tap a fiber-optic cable. Fiber-optic cable supports the transmission of voice, data, and video and is not subject to electrical interference. And if security is an issue, fiber-optic cable should be considered because tapping fiber-optic cable is difficult.

Two disadvantages of fiber-optic cable are cost and the installation expertise required.

Table 13-2 provides a summary of the four variations of Ethernet you can expect on the Networking Essentials exam.

Token Ring

A Token Ring network is a good choice for a network that has sustained moderate to heavy workloads.

A token ring network, using a star-wired ring topology, can operate at either 4 Mbps or 16 Mbps.

While 4-Mbps NICs operate only at 4 Mbps, 16-Mbps Token Ring network interface cards can usually be configured to run at either speed. If you are using one 4-Mbps NIC, all the other NICs on the network must be configured to operate at 4 Mbps. The network can only operate at one speed, either 4 Mbps or 16 Mbps.

Cabling choices for a token ring network are:

Table 13-2. The Maximum and Minimum Requirements for Ethernet Networks.

		Maximum workstations per segment	Maximum workstations per network[1]	Minimum cable length between workstations[2]	Maximum segment length	Maximum network distance
10BaseT	twisted pair	1	1024	2.5 meters (8 feet)	100 meters (328 feet)	not applicable
10Base2	coax ThinNet	30	90	0.5 meters (20 inches)	185 meters (607 feet)	925 meters (3035 feet)
10Base5	coax ThickNet	100	300	2.5 meters (8 feet)	500 meters (1640 feet)	2500 meters (8200 feet)
10BaseF	fiber optic	1	1024	not applicable	2000 meters (6562 feet)	not applicable

[1] An overall limitation of 1024 devices exists on any Ethernet network.
[2] On a 10BaseT network, the minimum cable length applies to the distance between the hub and the workstation.

Shielded twisted pair, also known as *IBM Type 1*

Unshielded twisted pair, also known as *IBM Type 3*

A hub known as a MSAU (multistation access unit) or MAU (media access unit) is located at the logical center of the ring and provides the ring topology.

ARCnet

ARCnet (*Attached Resource Computer network*) is an older form of LAN that has retained some popularity because of its simplicity. ARCnet has a slow transmission speed of 2.5 Mbps and supports a maximum of only 255 devices.

 ARCnet uses a RG-62 A/U 93-ohm coaxial cable.

For Review

- An Ethernet network uses CSMA/CD for media access control.
- There are four variations of 10-Mbps Ethernet.

10BaseT	twisted pair
10Base2	ThinNet
10Base5	ThickNet
10BaseF	fiber optic

- 10BaseT has a maximum cable length of 100 meters (328 feet) from the NIC to the hub and uses RJ-45 connectors.
- 10BaseT installations require twisted-pair cable with a minimum rating of category 3.
- Twisted-pair category 5 cable supports a data transfer rate up to 100 Mbps.
- 10Base2 has a maximum cable length of 185 meters (607) and supports up to 30 devices.
- 10Base2 uses RG-58 A/U coaxial cable with 50-ohm terminators.
- BNC connectors are used on a 10Basew2 network.
- 10Base2 and 10Base5 must be grounded on *only one end.*

■ 10Base5 has a maximum cable length of 500 meters and supports up to 100 devices.

■ AUI connectors are used on a 10Base5 network.

■ ARCnet uses a RG-62 A/U 93-ohm coaxial cable.

From Here

Chapter 3, "Transport Media," discussed the different categories of twisted-pair cables and Chapter 11, "Designing Your Network Architecture," had more information on media access mechanisms.

CHAPTER 14

Network Protocols

What Is a Protocol?

A *protocol* is like a language or a special vocabulary with a group of rules that a computer uses to communicate with other computers on a network. If you attempt to speak exclusively in Japanese (or Russian) to ordinary folks in the United States, you may not be able to communicate. Similarly, a computer attempting to use just one protocol, such as TCP/IP, with another computer that does not "know" TCP/IP, won't be able to communicate.

A *protocol suite* is a collection of protocols that are used together. It's reasonable to assume that protocols in the same suite should be compatible, and possibly even cooperate with each other. One example of a protocol suite is IPX and SPX, which were developed by Novell. To avoid the need to pay royalties to Novell, Microsoft created the Microsoft NWLink protocol. NWLink is completely compatible with and slightly faster than Novell's IPX/SPX suite. Microsoft is so proud of the NWLink IPX/SPX compatible protocol that Microsoft once used NWLink as the default protocol for Windows NT networks.

TIP
The Microsoft exam questions always refer to NWLink as *NWLink IPX/SPX compatible protocol*. NWLink is Microsoft's baby, and NWLink is

169

completely able to do all the work that IPX/SPX used to do on NetWare networks. NWLink is one of the methods Microsoft uses to ease the transition for companies switching from Novell networking to Microsoft networking.

Another example of a protocol suite is TCP/IP, which includes Internet Protocol (IP) and Transmission Control Protocol (TCP). The name TCP/IP rolls off the tongue so well that the compound name has stuck. The name TCP/IP also gives equal acknowledgment to the indispensable contributions of two protocol development groups who, together, created TCP and IP.

When two people do not speak in turn and simply shout at each other simultaneously, little communication takes place. Computers, of course, have the same difficulty. And one thing that protocols must do is to define when, and under what circumstances, each computer may communicate, and when each computer *may be expected* to communicate by other computers.

Computers use several varieties of protocols. At the lowest level of the OSI reference model you'll find protocols that define how the hardware speaks to other hardware.

When you install Windows NT Workstation software on a computer connected to a network, you must choose one or more protocols to use. Until Windows NT knows what protocol (rules) to obey, no communication with other computers on the network can occur. Unlike in humans, computer network protocols can easily be added or removed at any time after installation, using the Windows NT Control Panel Network Applet.

Your choice of protocols is important. Sometimes, the other computers that you intend to communicate with will determine the protocol required. At other times, the choice may also be left up to the network administrator. In every case, the choice must be based on several factors, including protocol speed, efficiency, and availability of that protocol on other systems.

TIP
Sometimes you must have special security or administrative privileges to have the right to install or modify existing protocols.

One factor that makes the protocol choice easier is Windows NT's ability to *bind,* or attach, multiple protocols to a single *network interface card* (NIC). When multiple protocols are in use on a network, the computer initiating communication attempts to use its "first priority" protocol. If the intended recipient computer can understand that first protocol, it will be used. If not, each successively bound protocol is tried until a common protocol is found.

The order of binding of protocols can greatly affect the performance of a network computer. During an attempt to establish communications with another computer, each protocol is tried in the binding order from top to bottom. The protocol most often used, or the most important protocol, generally should be moved to the top of the binding order list. (See Figure 14-1.)

Although multiple protocols can be bound to the same network card, this should only be done as necessary. Each additional protocol can slow down network performance because, as previously mentioned, each successive protocol is tried in each attempt to establish communication. Even at the bottom of the list, additional protocols use up valuable memory and overhead.

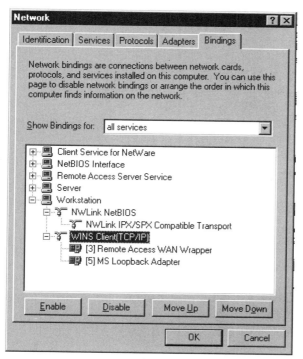

Fig. 14-1. Control Panel/Network applet's Bindings tab, where you can change the binding order.

For Review

- For two computers to communicate, each must use a matching protocol.

- NT can bind multiple protocols to a single network adapter.

- Binding order affects the order in which bound protocols are tried, in an attempt to find a common protocol between two computers before communications can occur.

Routable Protocols

Protocols can be broken down into two categories—those that can be routed and those that cannot. If a computer is on an isolated, freestanding network, then a nonroutable protocol may be an appropriate choice. However, if the network is connected to a second network, a routable protocol must be used for communication to take place across the connection between networks. Routable protocols carry addressing information to indicate which network the data is coming from and going to.

Most protocols used by Windows NT are routable. Two exceptions are Local Area Transport (LAT) protocol and NetBIOS Extended User Interface (NetBEUI) protocol, which are **not** routable. While LAT and NetBEUI can be used on a small network, once the network is expanded to include a router, the protocol must be switched to a routable protocol. The LAT protocol is used in a DEC/VAX environment.

TIP
The two most popular protocols for use with Microsoft networks are NetBEUI for nonroutable networks and TCP/IP for routable networks.

Frame Types

All data is transmitted in frames. A frame is made up of a header and data. The header includes such information as the source address and the destination address. The header can be organized in multiple ways. The way a frame header is organized defines a frame type.

Most protocols used by Windows NT use only one type of frame. On the other hand, NWLink uses several types of frames. The frame type does not need to be set for other protocols, but may well need to be set in the case of NWLink. This peculiarity of the NWLink protocol is highly likely to help you answer one or more test questions.

Transport Protocols

Transport protocols are used by Windows NT Workstation to communicate with other computers on a network. Each of these protocols can be installed via the network applet in the control panel.

NetBIOS Extended User Interface (NetBEUI)

NetBIOS Extended User Interface (NetBEUI) is the easiest protocol to install and use on Windows NT. (See Figure 14-2.) It is commonly seen in small office environments of 10 or fewer computers, particularly where there is not a computer-savvy staff.

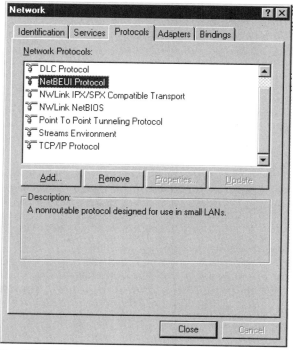

Fig. 14-2. The Control Panel/Network applet's Protocols tab, showing the NetBEUI protocol.

NetBEUI has two great advantages, speed and ease of installation. There are no options to choose when installing the NetBEUI protocol. Additionally, NetBEUI is one of the fastest protocols NT Workstation can use.

The major disadvantage of NetBEUI is that it cannot be routed. Because NetBEUI cannot be routed, it is limited in its usefulness to networks of around 20 computers or fewer.

TIP
Use of a bridge, router, or other connection to the Internet requires the binding of an additional protocol or a replacement of NetBEUI with a protocol that is routable.

IPX/SPX and NWLink IPX/SPX Compatible Transport

NWLink is Microsoft's answer to Novell's IPX/SPX protocol suite. Novell uses Internetwork Packet eXchange/Sequenced Packet eXchange (IPX/SPX) in its flagship product NetWare. Microsoft's NWLink is compatible with the original IPX/SPX suite and can communicate with computers using IPX. (In fact, independent tests have shown that NWLink is faster than the original IPX/SPX.) Additionally, when installing Client Services for NetWare (CSNW) or Gateway Services for NetWare (GSNW) on a Windows NT computer the NWLink protocol is automatically installed if it's not already on the workstation.

TIP
Installing NWLink IPX/SPX Compatible Transport on a Windows NT Workstation does not, by itself, allow the Windows NT Workstation to use file and print services on a Novell NetWare server. To use native Novell file and print services, either Microsoft's Client Services for NetWare must be installed on the Workstation, or the Workstation must access the NetWare server through a Windows NT Server that has Gateway Services for NetWare installed.

The IPX/SPX protocol suite uses the IPX protocol at the OSI network layer to handle connectionless transmissions. Common uses of this would be broadcast messages.

Sitting above IPX at the OSI transport layer is the SPX protocol. SPX is used for connection-based transmissions. SPX handles error checking, confirmation of transmission receipt, and retransmission of flawed data.

SERVICE ADVERTISING PROTOCOL

Another member protocol of the IPX/SPX protocol suite is the Service Advertising Protocol (SAP). SAP is used by servers to announce the availability of resources. A server with resources broadcasts a SAP packet announcing the available resources every 60 seconds. SAP resides at the session layer of the OSI reference model. Novell NetWare servers advertise their file server and print server services using SAP. This allows client computers to use SAP to determine what network resources are available to them.

Because SAP broadcasts can cause network congestion, especially over larger networks, Microsoft's NWLink does not make SAP broadcasts.

MICROSOFT FILE AND PRINT SERVICES FOR NETWARE

Novell is the most popular networking environment in the world. Microsoft wants to be the most popular. A step in the right direction, from that point of view, is the introduction of the first Microsoft Windows NT Server into any Novell network. The more Windows NT servers the better, of course, but the first one is the most significant step. To put its foot in the door, so to speak, Microsoft needed a way to get that first server into Novell networks. Microsoft File and Print Services for NetWare (FPNW) provides an ideal vehicle to accomplish this purpose.

File and Print Services for NetWare is a Windows NT server-based utility that allows the Microsoft server to look and function like a NetWare file and print server in a Novell network. This free adjunct service is available for installation on any Windows NT server, so any Windows NT server can join and interoperate with a Novell network by sharing the Windows NT Server's directories and printers.

Of course, any Microsoft Windows NT client or Windows 95 client computers on the network can still access and use the service of the Windows NT server at the same time that the server appears to Novell clients to be a Novell server. So there is no loss in service to any clients by adding this service to a Novell network. In fact, it adds services by allowing Microsoft clients to access NetWare printers.

INSTALLING NWLINK

When NWLink is installed on a Windows NT Workstation, two new entries to the network protocols list will be available:

NWLink IPX/SPX Compatible Transport and NWLink NetBIOS. Only the IPX/SPX Compatible Transport has any configurable properties. The two choices required during installation of NWLink are to select the frame type and enter the NetWare network number (see Figure 14-3). These choices are explained in the next three paragraphs.

NETWARE NETWORK NUMBER

The network number is an eight-digit hexadecimal number that is set by the network administrator and is associated with the network cable and all the computers on it. The number is bound to the specific network adapter that is attached to the cable, not the NetWare server itself. Thus every NetWare server and workstation attached to the same cable must have the same number associated with the network adapter attached to the cable to communicate.

NETWARE FRAME TYPES

The IPX protocol allows the use of several types of frame. The frame type describes the type of headers that are added to data prior to transmission. Windows NT supports four frame types for IPX with Ethernet:

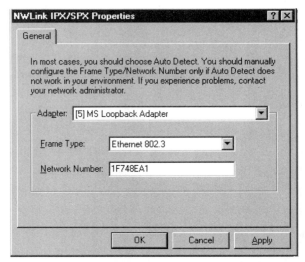

Fig. 14-3. Installing the NWLink protocol entails entering the network number and possibly setting a frame type.

- 802.2

- 802.3

- Ethernet II

- Ethernet SNAP (SubNetwork Access Protocol)

Windows NT supports two frame types in a Token Ring environment. An administrator can choose between Token Ring and Token Ring SNAP.

The frame type should be set to Auto Detect initially. This will automatically set the frame type and the second property setting, network number, based on the traffic that is detected on the network when the workstation is started. If no traffic or a mix of traffic is detected, the frame type and network number must be manually set. The frame type must also match between all computers that wish to communicate.

MISMATCHED FRAME TYPES—802.3 VERSUS 802.2

A major cause of problems on an IPX network is mismatched frame types. Novell NetWare versions prior to 3.12 used Ethernet 802.3 as default. NetWare 3.12 and later versions use Ethernet 802.2 as default. One of the simplest ways to avoid frame type mismatches is to ensure that all NetWare servers are manually set to the same frame type. If an entire network already uses a frame type other than the default (802.2 for Windows NT), the frame type on a client computer new to the network must be set to match the network.

NWLink, in addition to its ease of connecting to NetWare servers, is faster than TCP/IP and easier to configure.

NWLink has disadvantages compared to both NetBEUI and TCP/IP. NetBEUI is fast and needs no configuration. NWLink has no hierarchical numbering scheme as does TCP/IP. While this is fine in smaller networks, connecting in a WAN environment becomes a major challenge.

For Review

- NWLink is routable and faster than TCP/IP.

- The network number and frame type must match between two computers before communications using NWLink can occur.

- NWLink is needed for communications with a NetWare server.

- NWLink does not have a standardized number scheme like TCP/IP does.

TCP/IP

The *Transmission Control Protocol/Internet Protocol* (TCP/IP) suite is used on the world's largest network of networks, the Internet.

AN INTERNET TIME CAPSULE

The Internet (then called the ARPANET, circa 1969) was originally developed by the U.S.A. Defense Advanced Research Projects Agency (DARPA). Its first application was as part of a project to interconnect Defense-funded supercomputer research centers. The earliest mission of the Internet was provided by the U.S.A. education and research community's interest in communication, collaboration, data sharing, and resource sharing.

The Defense Communications Agency (DCA) began control of the ARPANET in 1975, and later, in 1983, the Defense Data Network (MILNET) split away from ARPANET, leaving the Internet an ostensibly civilian, government, and higher education project.

Throughout the 1980s, the Internet grew rapidly as various government agencies and sundry institutions of higher learning scrambled to join in. Because of their power, flexibility, and extreme durability in mission-critical production environments, UNIX computers were increasingly used to connect local campuses and networks to the Net.

By 1990 the Advanced Research Projects Agency (ARPA) ceased any control of the Internet, and the United States National Science Foundation (NSF) took over Internet funding and guidance.

In 1993, with the simultaneous popularity of a powerful Hypertext Transfer Protocol (HTTP), Graphical User Interfaces (GUIs), and the advent of slick multiprotocol browsers (like *Netscape Communicator*® and *Internet Explorer*®) on the World Wide Web, TCP/IP expanded the use of the Internet to businesses and households worldwide.

Almost immediately, in 1995, the NSF Internet Backbone was decommissioned, and private funding of the Net quickly displaced government funding.

TCP/IP was first used on the Internet in 1983. TCP/IP is designed to work over almost all known communication media:

Ethernet

Token Ring

Telephone

Cellular

Microwave

Satellite

Shortwave radio

To install TCP/IP requires the minimum following settings:

IP address

Subnet mask

Default gateway (if the network is routed)

See Figure 14-4.

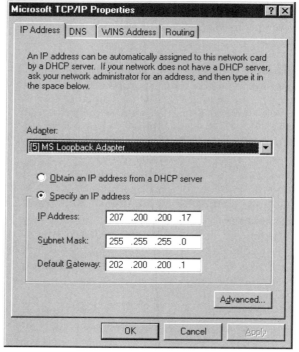

Fig. 14-4. TCP/IP Properties IP Address tab in Windows NT.

TIP

For the Networking Essentials examination, you should also consider a setting for "default gateway" to be at least an *important* setting, if not an *essential* setting. Some networks do require the default gateway to be set for Internet access to succeed—other networks do not. If a network operates as a routed environment, the default gateway is an essential setting. If the network is not routed, the default gateway is not an essential setting.

If the exam question requires two answers, remember the IP address and subnet mask must be known for the computer to participate on the network. If three answers are needed, assume you're dealing with a routed environment and add the default gateway to the list of required settings.

The IP address is a unique address assigned to the computer. The subnet mask breaks the IP address into a network portion and a host or node portion. If a message needs to go to a different network than the originating network, it is routed to the destination network through the default gateway.

The DNS tab allows an administrator to configure the Domain Name System (DNS) settings for the protocol. DNS translates from Internet names to IP addresses. (See Figure 14-5.)

TIP

Do not confuse Internet domains with Windows NT domains. Internet domains, such as Microsoft.Com, consist of a group of computers that have the same subnet mask and network address portion of their IP address. A Windows NT domain defines a group of computers connected to a Windows NT Server acting as a Domain Controller and controlling security for that Windows NT domain.

Windows Internet Name Services (WINS) is a Microsoft protocol that helps track and resolve computer names on a network. Additionally, WINS can work with DNS in resolving Internet names to computer addresses. (See Figure 14-6.)

The greatest advantage of TCP/IP is its continued growth as a worldwide de facto standard. For compatibility with the Internet, many businesses are choosing this protocol as a standard. Additionally, the addressing scheme allows each computer connected to the Internet to be uniquely identified.

If a network does not need Internet access, TCP/IP may not be the protocol of choice. TCP/IP requires more configuration than other protocols NT Workstation uses, either on each client computer or on a separate Dynamic Host Configuration Protocol (DHCP) server. Also, NWLink and NetBEUI both run quicker than TCP/IP.

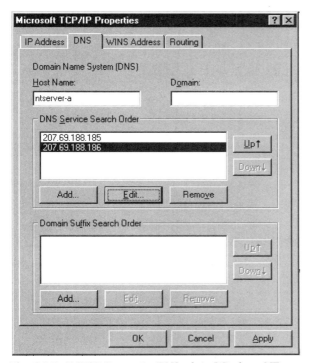

Fig. 14-5. TCP/IP Properties DNS tab in Windows NT.

For Review

- TCP/IP is the primary protocol suite used on the Internet.

- Although slow and complex to configure, TCP/IP offers a wealth of optional settings.

- DHCP can be used to centralize and ease configuration of workstations.

- DNS and WINS are used to allow the use of human-friendly text addresses rather than IP addresses.

AppleTalk

AppleTalk was developed by Apple Computer as the protocol suite for use with its Macintosh products. It was originally designed for use in small networks and has been expanded by Apple to handle networks as large as 16 million nodes. Due to its being built into

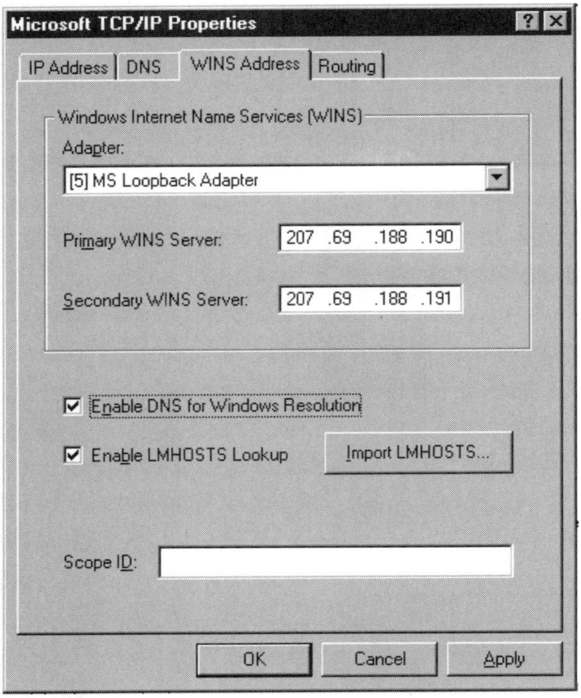

Microsoft TCP/IP Properties

IP Address | DNS | WINS Address | Routing

Windows Internet Name Services (WINS)

Adapter:

[5] MS Loopback Adapter

Primary WINS Server: 207 .69 .188 .190

Secondary WINS Server: 207 .69 .188 .191

☑ Enable DNS for Windows Resolution

☑ Enable LMHOSTS Lookup   Import LMHOSTS...

Scope ID:

OK   Cancel   Apply

Fig. 14-6. TCP/IP WINS Address tab in Windows NT.

each Macintosh computer shipped, without requiring a separate network card purchase, it has become the overwhelming leader of Apple networking. AppleTalk provides stability and reliable delivery through the AppleTalk transaction protocol (ATP) located at the OSI transport layer. ATP employs socket-to-socket transmissions, requiring both a transaction request and a transaction response.

The default zone must be set when using AppleTalk. AppleTalk networks are divided into zones. Zones are logical divisions of network resources and each zone has a name.

AppleTalk is a required protocol if Macintosh computers are to be included on a network. Client Services for Macintosh must be installed to allow Macintosh computers to share files and printers with Windows NT computers.

However, AppleTalk is slow. At 230.4 Kbps, AppleTalk is rarely used as a primary protocol in larger networks.

See Figure 14-7.

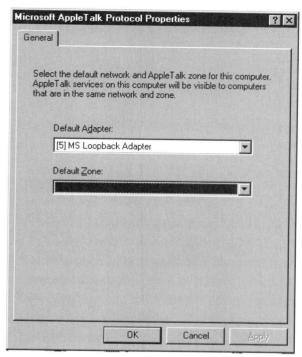

Fig. 14-7. AppleTalk Configuration in Windows NT.

Data Link Control (DLC) Protocol

Data Link Control (DLC) Protocol allows Windows NT to communicate with some older IBM mainframes and use direct network printing on some Hewlett-Packard (HP) and Lexmark printers. Newer HP printers use TCP/IP to communicate.

There are no parameters to be set for DLC.

DLC is not routable, making it the third nonroutable protocol available on a Windows NT network. (REMINDER: The other two nonroutable protocols are NetBEUI and LAT. Please remember these three in a special, warm part of your heart.)

The only advantage of using the DLC protocol is allowing a computer to communicate with an already installed IBM mainframe or an HP or Lexmark printer connected directly to the network.

See Figure 14-8.

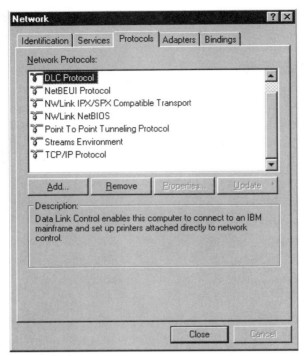

Fig. 14-8. The Control Panel Network applet's Protocols tab, showing the DLC protocol.

STREAMS

The STREAMS Environment Protocol enables transport drivers developed in the STREAMS environment to port to Windows NT. This protocol is not used unless you are connecting a Windows NT network to a UNIX computer running STREAMS.

Dial-up Protocols

When a user is remotely dialing into the network, a dial-up protocol is used. Serial Line Internet Protocol (SLIP) and Point-to-Point Protocol (PPP) are the two major dial-up protocols. SLIP is the older and more primitive of the two protocols. PPP offers additional error checking and other, newer features.

SLIP does not provide an automatic IP address number for TCP/IP applications to use in interacting on the Internet. The newer PPP protocol can provide an automatic IP address upon connection to the Internet, which allows TCP/IP applications (such as Web browsers or WHOIS service) to interact with other Internet-connected computers.

POINT-TO-POINT TUNNELING PROTOCOL (PPTP)

Windows NT also offers the Point-to-Point Tunneling Protocol (PPTP). PPTP is a network protocol that enables the secure transfer of data from a remote client to a server by creating a virtual private network (VPN). This is performed across a TCP/IP-based data network, usually the Internet. This method allows the transfer of other protocols, such as NetBEUI, across the Internet. This is accomplished by encrypting and encapsulating the original packet to make it appear as a PPP packet. The main benefit of PPTP is private transfer of data across a public network.

Other Protocols

X.25

X.25 is a standard packet-switched network communications protocol used for WANs. Some organizations use the X.25 protocol over an elaborate worldwide network or packet forwarding nodes called Data Communications Equipment nodes (DCEs). After the X.25 protocol has been installed, a Windows NT Workstation can use the X.25 protocol either by creating a dial-up networking connection to an X.25 Packet Assembler/Dissembler (PAD) service, or by adding an X.25 hardware network card and connecting a cable directly from an X.25 network.

ROUTING INFORMATION PROTOCOL (RIP)

Routing Information Protocol (RIP) is a network layer protocol used to route network traffic. Each routing device keeps a routing table and broadcasts the table at regular intervals. Other routing devices listen for other routing table broadcasts and update their own tables. Routers then use these tables to choose a path when routing data from source to destination.

RIP protocol updating is performed using a vector distance algorithm to choose optimum routes. RIP is used with both NetWare and in TCP/IP.

SERVER MESSAGE BLOCK (SMB) PROTOCOL

The Server Message Block (SMB) Protocol operates at the OSI application layer. SMB is characterized by a block of data that contains client/server requests or responses. The SMB Protocol is used in all areas of Microsoft network communication, and was developed originally by Microsoft, Intel, and IBM.

NETWORK FILE SYSTEM (NFS) PROTOCOL

The Network File System (NFS) Protocol was developed by SUN Microsystems and is used primarily in UNIX computers. UNIX computers commonly share files using NFS on TCP/IP networks. Using NFS may become necessary if a UNIX workstation has shared files that must be accessed by Windows NT computers, or if UNIX workstations must have access to shared files on a Windows NT computer.

TWO WAYS TO ACCOMPLISH NETWORK COMMUNICATION

Connectionless Communication Service

Connectionless communication service doesn't guarantee that the intended recipient receives the message transmitted by the sender. There is no preexisting connection between the sending computer and receiving computer(s). The receiving computer does not send an acknowledgment if or when the message arrives. Even if the message is received, with connectionless service there is no way to check if the message arrived free of errors. A message broadcasted to all, or many, users might use a connectionless communication service, if it is not mission critical that every user receive the message.

Connection-Oriented Communication Service

Connection-oriented communication service ensures reliable communications between two computers, including prevention of data loss or corruption. A communication connection is established between the sending computer and the receiving computer. After each communication transaction, the receiving computer sends an acknowledgment to the sending computer that the message was received. For example, File Transfer Protocol (FTP) uses the TCP portion of TCP/IP for connection-oriented, reliable file transfers.

Performance of connection-oriented communication is often improved by using a sliding window algorithm. Initially, setting the send window size to be larger than the receive window size will provide better network performance. The window size on the sending computer defines the number of packets that can be sent before an acknowledgment must be received. The window size on the receiving computer defines the number of packets that can be received before an acknowledgment must be sent. The combination of these two settings allows the sending computer to continue sending packets while receiving less-frequent acknowledgments.

PART FOUR

Implementation

Chapter 15, "Taming the Human Part," discusses the User Manager for Domains application in Windows NT 4.0 Server.

Chapter 16, "Taming the Hardware," provides MCSE candidates with preparation for the Networking Essentials exam questions about hardware installation and troubleshooting. In particular, this chapter discusses resolving hardware interrupt conflicts.

Chapter 17, "Taming the Network," covers a variety of network problems including attenuation, broadcast storms, and packet collisions, and reviews collision detection, collision avoidance, and token passing media access control schemes. This chapter also reviews network segmentation devices.

Chapter 18, "Node Addressing," discusses a variety of computer naming systems that coexist on today's networks. This chapter reviews the naming systems from the point of view of the Networking Essentials examination.

CHAPTER 15

Taming the Human Part

This chapter discusses the User Manager for Domains application in Windows NT 4.0 Server. User Manager for Domains is found under Administrative Tools in the Program group on the Start menu.

Network administrators are required to control human interactions with the network. The administrator has security concerns, access concerns, convenience concerns, turnover concerns, obsolescence concerns, etc. User Manager for Domains consolidates many powerful functions that network administrators need everyday, making it a popular and useful tool.

User Manager for Domains

With User Manager for Domains an administrator can

- Create user accounts.

- Modify or rename user accounts.

- Disable user accounts.

- Delete user accounts.

- Check user account information.

- Create global group accounts and local group accounts.
- Add user accounts to groups.
- Set security policies.
- Grant rights and permissions to user accounts and group accounts.

 User Manager for Domains, shown in Figure 15-1, provides a powerful tool for managing user accounts and access to network resources.

When Windows NT is installed, two built-in user accounts are automatically created:

Administrator

Guest

The Administrator account allows the administrator to perform many domain management functions, including managing user accounts and group accounts.

Users who do not have an account on the network may use the Guest account. For security, when Windows NT is installed, the Guest account is disabled.

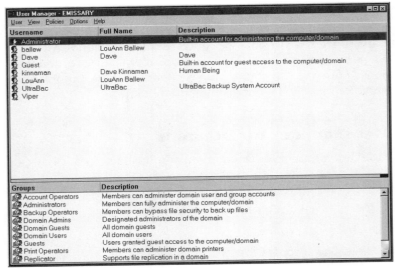

Fig. 15-1. User Manager for Domains displays domain users and groups.

Creating New User Accounts

For a user to log onto the network, they must log in as a guest or have a user account. The New User dialog box in User Manager for Domains (Figure 15-2) is used to create new user accounts.

NEW USER INFORMATION

When establishing a new user account, the following information can be entered:

- Username
- Full name
- Description
- Password
- Confirm Password

NEW USER OPTIONS

As applicable, the following options also may be checked:

- User Must Change Password at Next Logon
- User Cannot Change Password
- Password Never Expires
- Account Disabled

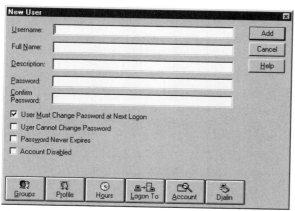

Fig. 15-2. New users are added in this dialog box in User Manager for Domains.

Selecting **User Must Change Password at Next Logon** requires a user to change the password at his or her first logon.

Selecting **User Cannot Change Password** prevents a user from changing the password.

Selecting **Password Never Expires** is a useful setting for certain accounts where it is not desirable to have a changing password. Accounts that represent installed services or guest accounts without security access rights are often set to *Password Never Expires*.

Selecting **Account Disabled** disables the account so that it cannot be used.

For more information on passwords see "Account (Password) Policy," below.

NEW USER TABS
There are six tabs available from the New User dialog box:

Groups

Profile

Hours

Logon To

Account

Dialin

Groups
From the Groups tab, the administrator can access the Group Memberships screen shown in Figure 15-3. Administrators use Group Memberships to add specific users to one or more available groups, or to remove a user from one or more groups.

Profile
By clicking on the Profile tab, the administrator can go to the User Environment Profile dialog box shown in Figure 15-4 and set User Profiles and Home Directory.

The User Profile Path provides a path to a folder where information about the user's desktop environment is stored. Retaining this information allows a user's specific environment settings to be loaded during logon.

The Logon Script Name within the User Profiles section points to an executable file that runs when the user logs onto the network.

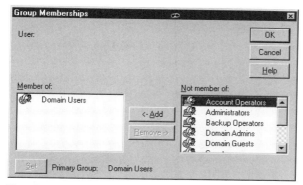

Fig. 15-3. User accounts are added to Groups from the Group Memberships dialog box.

A home directory is a personal directory for a single user. A home directory is a private directory, containing the user's files and perhaps programs that a user controls.

Hours
Logon Hours, shown in Figure 15-5, is available through the Hours tab and provides an administrator the ability to allow or disallow specific hours for the user to log onto the network. The default is to allow access 24 hours a day, seven days a week.

Logon To
An administrator can allow a user access to all workstations or restrict the user to specifically named workstations through the Logon Workstations dialog box available from the Logon To tab. The Logon Workstations dialog box is shown in Figure 15-6.

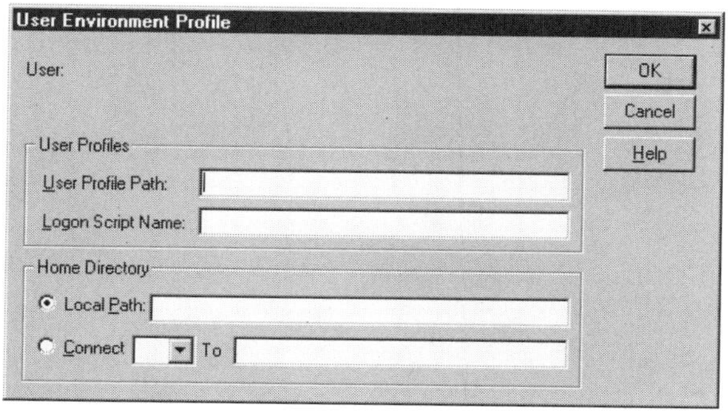

Fig. 15-4. A User Environment Profile in User Manager for Domains.

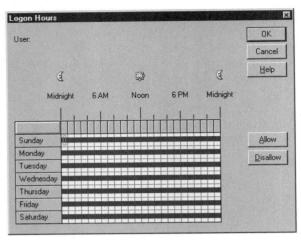

Fig. 15-5. Specific Logon Hours can be allowed or disallowed for individual accounts.

Account

From the Account Information screen, shown in Figure 15-7, accessed from the Account tab, an administrator can set the account to expire never or on a specific date. The Account Type, Global or Local, can also be set from this screen. The default is global account type.

By setting a specific date for account expiration, accounts for temporary employees can be automatically disabled so the accounts are not kept active for longer than necessary.

Logon Workstations

User:

◉ User May Log On To All Workstations
○ User May Log On To These Workstations

OK
Cancel
Help

1		5	
2		6	
3		7	
4		8	

Fig. 15-6. A user can be restricted to specific workstations by using the Logon Workstations dialog box.

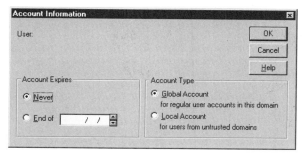

Fig. 15-7. The Account screen in User Manager for Domains.

Dialin

The Dialin Information screen, shown in Figure 15-8, accessed from the Dialin tab, allows individual user accounts to be given permission or denied permission to dial in to the server. If dial-in permission is given, the server may be required to call the user back as an additional security, expense, or convenience measure.

Creating New Group Accounts

From the User Menu in User Manager for Domains, New Global Group or New Local Group can be selected. The New Global Group dialog box is shown in Figure 15-9 and the New Local Group dialog box is shown in Figure 15-10.

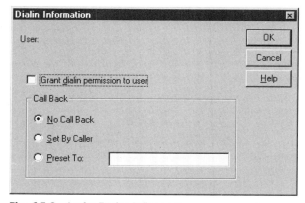

Fig. 15-8. At the Dialin Information screen remote access permission can be set for each user account.

Each group contains user accounts, called Members. Because a group can be granted rights and permissions, creating special purpose groups is a convenient way to aggregate similar user accounts to allow each member of the group the same rights and permissions.

In other words, rather than assigning rights and permissions to each and every user account created one-by-one, add the user account to a predefined group that already has appropriate rights and permissions. This technique is especially handy when the time arrives to change one of the permissions. By changing the group's permissions, you effectively change the permissions of each member of the group.

When Windows NT 4.0 Server is installed, several built-in group accounts are automatically installed, including:

- Built-in global groups

   Domain administrators

   Domain users

   Domain guests

- Built-in local groups (may access only the home domain)

   Administrator

   Server operators

   Account operators

   Print operators

The differences between local and global groups are more complex than immediately meets the eye. First, note that local groups may access resources *only* in their home domain. Local groups are appropriate for use, then, in resource domains that offer files and services over the network.

Global groups have potentially wider access. In a large multidomain organization, global groups may have specific access rights in more than one domain.

One or more global groups can be included within a local group. Local groups cannot include other local groups. Global groups cannot contain anything except users—no global or local groups may be included in a global group.

NEW GLOBAL GROUP ACCOUNTS

To create a new global group, provide a Group Name and add the appropriate user accounts. In a large organization, global groups

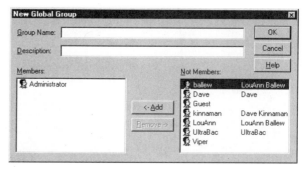

Fig. 15-9. The New Global Group dialog box in User Manager for Domains.

are not necessarily limited to access only in the domain where they are created.

NEW LOCAL GROUP ACCOUNTS

To create a new local group, provide a Group Name and add users and global group accounts. A local group provides access to resources *only* in the domain where the local group was created.

Account (Password) Policy

Controlling use of passwords is an important part of the overall security plan of a network. The Account Policy, as shown in Figure 15-11, is available through the Policies menu in User Manager for Domain by selecting Account. Account Policy controls how passwords are used on the network by user accounts.

Fig. 15-10. The New Local Group dialog box in User Manager for Domains.

Account Policy allows an administrator to set password restrictions regarding:

- Maximum password age
- Minimum password age
- Minimum password length
- Password uniqueness

The account policy can be set so an account will be locked out after a specified number of unsuccessful logon attempts. A locked account cannot log onto the network.

The account policy can also be set so users who exceed their logon hours are forcibly disconnected from the network. Logon hours are set from the Hours tab on the New User screen.

If Users Must Log On In Order To Change Password is selected, a user who does not change his or her password before the password expires will require assistance from the administrator to regain access to the network.

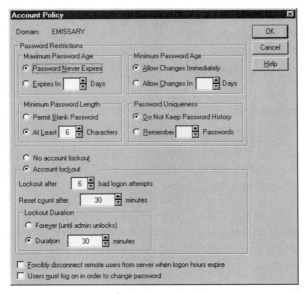

Fig. 15-11. Account Policy provides for various password restrictions and settings.

User Rights

User Rights, as shown in Figure 15-12, can be set through the Policies menu in User Manager for Domain after selecting User Rights. When the administrator grants a right to a user account or a group account, that account is allowed to perform certain activities on the network. A granted right applies to activities networkwide, and a granted permission applies only to a specific object.

Audit Policy

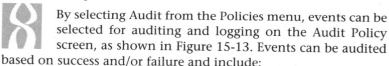 By selecting Audit from the Policies menu, events can be selected for auditing and logging on the Audit Policy screen, as shown in Figure 15-13. Events can be audited based on success and/or failure and include:

- Logon and logoff
- File and object access
- Use of user rights
- User and group management
- Security policy changes
- Restart, shutdown, and system
- Process tracking

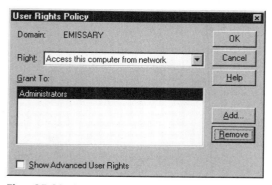

Fig. 15-12. User Rights can be granted to user accounts and group accounts with the User Rights Policy dialog box.

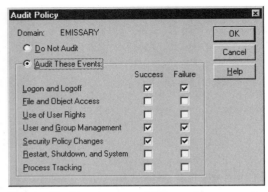

Fig. 15-13. The success and failure of events can be audited by the Audit Policy in User Manager for Domains.

 Audit policy results are logged to the security log. The security log is only available to System Administrators and is accessed through the Event Viewer located in Administrative Tools under the Programs Group from the Start menu.

An audit entry provides information about the type of event logged, the user, the date, and the time of the event.

For Review

- User Manager for Domains can be used to manage user accounts and access to the network.

- Group accounts are a convenient way of grouping user accounts.

- For security, set password restrictions in Account Policy.

- Auditing events provides information on who used audited network resources.

- The security log in Event Viewer allows an administrator to view audited events.

CHAPTER 16

Taming the Hardware

The Networking Essentials examination, like all Microsoft MCSE exams, focuses on common, ordinary, everyday aspects of administration and support of computer hardware and software. This chapter covers just such an ordinary task in everyday networking: replacing a hardware card in a x86 computer.

Now, what hardware card shall our common, ordinary example be? We *are* talking about networked computers, right? What hardware card do networked computers have in common, that is just as ordinary as a video card or a keyboard, for networked computers? Right! We're going to replace the network interface card, the NIC. All God's children got shoes, and all networked computers got NICs. In this chapter, we're going to fix a NIC.

In the implementation section of the official Microsoft online preparation guide for the Networking Essentials exam, this standard for MCSE knowledge is stated: "Given the manufacturer's documentation for the network adapter, install, configure, and resolve hardware conflicts for multiple network adapters in a token-ring or Ethernet network."

Information in this chapter prepares you to satisfy that standard as it is tested on the exam by demonstrating the process with a single Ethernet adapter card. Installing multiple adapters in a single computer is more time consuming and complicated; however, the same procedures are used in repetition.

Hardware Installations and Repairs

Keeping in mind that most common network problems are corrected by attention to cabling and/or connectors, here are some initial questions to ask as you begin to tame the hardware on a network. We are, in this example, trying to figure out what's wrong when a user has no network access.

Is the problem hardware, software, or user?

- Did the computer work before?
- Did the problem begin recently?
- What changed between when it worked and when it failed?
- How many computers are experiencing the problem?
- Has hardware or software been installed?
- Have computers or cabling been moved?
- Do the cables run near sources of electrical interference, such as fluorescent lights?
- Has the network been changed?
- When it worked, did the computer have other software?
- When it worked, did the network have other protocols or services?
- Are the transmit/receive data lights on the NIC lit, blinking, or dark?

CAUTION
Before delving into any hardware problem, be sure to make appropriate backup copies of all system configuration files.

In Windows NT 4.0, that means before you change systems setting, or install software or hardware, you should make a fresh ERD (*rdisk /s*), and save the partition information from the Programs | Administrative Tools | Disk Administrator | Partition | Configuration menu.

With these two disks safely labeled and dated, you are in a better position to restore a Windows NT computer to at least its current condition, if anything goes terribly wrong.

Start Simple

First, check the cables. Regardless of the reason, check for yourself to see if the cable has been removed from the NIC. Does the cable only appear to be in place? If the network is a 10BaseT Ethernet twisted-pair network, remove and reseat the RJ-45 connector in the NIC. Listen for or feel the click as it fits into place. Check the other end of the cable, too. Is the span of the cable visibly crimped or damaged? Are the RJ-45 connectors firmly attached?

If new hardware or software was recently installed on the computer or the network, settings may have been changed in that installation and configuration process, thereby causing the problem. Consider removing or disabling the new hardware or software, to see if the problem vanishes. Consider restoring the computer's setting from the backup configuration you made before the new hardware or software was installed.

Shut down the computer. Power off. Wait. Reboot. Watch for error messages while the computer is rebooting.

Assuming the network card is still not working, there may be an interrupt conflict. Interrupts (called *IRQs*) are used by devices to signal the computer's CPU that they are ready for the CPU's attention. In general, each device must have its own unique interrupt channel to the CPU, so that two devices do not use the same IRQ at the same time.

Plug-and-Play systems and devices were invented, at least partially, to solve these resource conflicts with minimal human intervention. Until Plug-and-Play has been perfected and universally deployed, there will be IRQ conflicts for computer technicians to resolve.

Verify Network Card Settings

Use the Windows NT Control Panel Network applet, or the Windows 95/98 Control Panel System Properties applet to check the network card and its settings. The Windows NT Network applet is shown in Figure 16-1. Write down the settings and compare them to that computer's journal and/or the network database entry for that computer—have the IRQ settings and/or I/O port base settings been changed without updating the database or the journal?

Use the diagnostic or configuration software that came with the network card, or in Windows NT use the Control Panel Network applet, or, in Windows 95/98 go to Control Panel | System | Device Manager | Properties (as shown in Figure 16-2) to check the network adapter card resource settings.

If the broken computer has a Windows NT Workstation operating system, check the IRQ settings using Windows NT Diagnostics on the Administrative Tools menu, as shown in Figure 16-3.

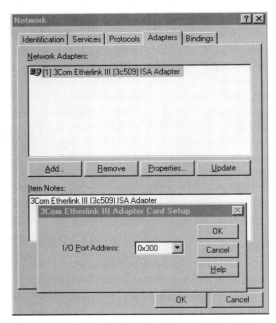

Fig. 16-1. Use Windows NT Control Panel Network Applet to observe and adjust the I/O port base address of the network card.

Check with the manufacturer's Internet site to see if there is more recent diagnostic software, or more appropriate network card drivers available. Confirm the card's available IRQ settings and I/O base settings from the original network card manual or from the manufacturer's Web site.

ThinNet Trials

If the network is 10Base2 (ThinNet) Ethernet, try connecting two working computers with a cable, T-connectors, and good terminators. If the two good computers can both see each other, then remove the cable from one of the good computers and connect it to the broken computer. If the broken computer and the good computer can now see each other, the cabling and/or connectors for the "bad" computer are at fault.

Put a 50-ohm terminator directly onto the BNC connector on the broken computer's network card. If the computer can now see itself, some type of cabling and/or connector problem exists. It

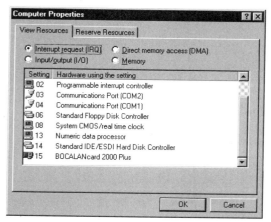

Fig. 16-2. Check IRQS, I/O ports, DMA and Memory from this screen.

could be an electrical short in the cabling, improper termination, or mismatched cabling.

It never hurts to verify that you have the right kind of cabling, terminators, and/or connectors for the network. Confirm that only 50-ohm terminators are used at each end of the network bus,

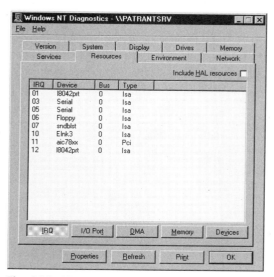

Fig. 16-3. Use the Windows NT Diagnostics Applet on the Administrative Tools menu to check the computer's IRQs.

and that only the correct RG-58 A/U cabling is in use. Make sure that the correct T-connectors are firmly connected to each network card.

Network Adapter Card Interrupts

The IRQ that you assign to a network adapter card must be unique. No other device may also use that same IRQ. IRQ2 and IRQ9 are generally not available. The typical default or standard assignments for IRQs in x86-based computers are shown in Table 16-1.

Table 16-1. Note the IRQs That Are Commonly Available: IRQ3, IRQ5, IRQ10, IRQ11, IRQ12, IRQ15.

Default Interrupt Requests—IRQs	Typical Device (possible use)
0	timer
1	keyboard
2	2-9 cascade, Video Card EGA/VGA
3	available (serial port COM2 or COM4)
4	COM1 or COM3
5	available (LPT2 or sound card or NIC)
6	floppy disk controller
7	parallel port (LPT1)
8	real-time clock
9	redirected IRQ2
10	available
11	available
12	available (PS/2 mouse)
13	math coprocessor
14	hard disk controller
15	available

To demonstrate how to use Table 16-1, here is an example. Say you want to install the new network card on IRQ3. Which device does Table 16-1 predict would possibly cause a conflict over IRQ3? The correct answer is COM2, or possibly COM4, because they typically are automatically enabled and assigned IRQ3. COM2 is probably already automatically assigned IRQ3. This fact is also acknowledged by Microsoft in TechNet, "If you have two or more COM ports on your computer, you might find that a network adapter card . . . will conflict with one port."

For the Networking Essentials examination, it is probably not necessary to memorize the entire IRQ table. However, most MCSEs are quite familiar with the IRQ table in their daily travails, so MCSE candidates should become familiar with the entire table. In applying the IRQ table, note that it is particularly valuable to know that some IRQs are more likely than others to be available when a new device is being installed.

Available IRQs are an important resource. The IRQs typically available for a newly installed hardware card, from Table 16-1, are IRQ3, IRQ5, IRQ10, IRQ11, IRQ12, and IRQ15. These are the first IRQ choices to use in installing a new NIC.

The Networking Essentials exam seems to concentrate on the lower half of the standard IRQ range shown in Table 16-1, and many exam candidates focus on memorizing the range of IRQ2 through IRQ7. Such an abbreviated IRQ table is shown as Table 16-2.

Disabling Ports to Free IRQs

Although it is not necessarily a simple process, it is often possible to disable one or more unused resources, such as ports, to free IRQs for alternate assignments.

Built-in serial or parallel ports can be disabled on most Intel x86-based computers. However, it would be a mistake to assign an IRQ to a network card if that IRQ is already assigned to an active serial or parallel port, even if no device is physically attached to the port. Although built-in serial or parallel ports can be disabled, it may not be the simplest available option.

To disable a port you may be required to adjust the BIOS or CMOS of the computer, and/or adjust the basic port settings through the operating system Control Panel. After a port is disabled, the IRQ that the port previously used may be reassigned to another device, such as a network card.

Table 16-2.
Abbreviated IRQ Table Includes IRQ2 Through IRQ7.

Device	IRQ
Video	IRQ2
COM2, 4	IRQ3*
COM1, 3	IRQ4
LPT2	IRQ5*
Floppy	IRQ6
LPT1	IRQ7

* NOTE: In the abbreviated range from IRQ2 to IRQ7, only IRQ3 and IRQ5 are typically available. IRQ3 may be available *if the communication port(s) COM2 or COM4
on the computer are disabled.* IRQ 5 is typically available because x86 computers
rarely require a second parallel printer port, making LPT2 unnecessary and, therefore, making IRQ5 available for a sound card, a NIC, or some other additional card.

As an example, what if a computer uses only remote network
printers? There is no need on that computer for LPT1 or LPT2,
because the operating system redirector sends print jobs out over
the NIC. So, if you find it necessary, you may want to disable the
built-in parallel printer ports for both LPT1 and LPT2, thus making IRQ5 and IRQ7 available for other uses.

As another example, what if the computer has a PS/2 mouse, a
modem on COM1, and you need to install a network card? By disabling the unused COM2 port, you could potentially free IRQ3 for
use with the NIC. In this same example, if the computer has no
sound card, it's likely that IRQ5 is also available. IRQ5 is sometimes designated as a preferred IRQ for network cards, so it might
be worth a try. If you do run into difficulty with the NIC on IRQ5,
note from Table 16-1 that the problem is probably a conflict with
LPT2 or a Sound Card.

But *why bother* with changing the CMOS, fighting with motherboard Plug-and-Play, and Control Panel settings to disable the
COM2 port? There are probably other available IRQs, such as
IRQ10, IRQ11, and IRQ15, so you don't need to take the extra
effort to disable the COM2 port to free up IRQ3, even though you

probably could. Try to use the other, higher IRQs first, to keep the job simple.

Resolve IRQ Conflicts

One of the first principles of computer hardware repair is to start from what works and make tiny changes, one at a time, to see if the situation improves. If the most recent tiny change does not improve things, reverse that tiny change and confirm that you have not lost capability in the experiment. Then try a different tiny change. By repeating this process slowly and painfully you can know that, at least, you haven't made things worse.

Changing IRQs is often similar to the process just described. You may be required to coordinate and verify IRQ changes at the BIOS/CMOS, Plug-and-Play, Control Panel, and in the manufacturer's configuration software. If you're lucky, the various settings will be stable and identical, and there will be no conflict with IRQs used by other devices.

The two foremost requirements of resolving network card IRQ conflicts are these:

1. There must be an unassigned interrupt available for the network card to use.

2. The available interrupt must be compatible with the network card.

Use the Windows NT Diagnostics applet or the Windows 95/98 Control Panel System applet to check the IRQ resources already in use. In Windows 98, System Information in the Tools menu can also be used to view IRQ settings and conflicts. Compare the settings in use with Table 16-1, and locate one or more IRQs that are possibly available. Try these first. It may be necessary to try more than one IRQ before you find one that is truly available.

Setting or Changing the IRQ

Depending on the NIC involved, you may be able to set or change the IRQ using software; or, especially on older and more primitive cards, you may need to set a jumper switch on the physical card itself. Some cards have only a certain few available settings, so that you must find an IRQ that is both available and compatible with that card.

In Windows 95/98, set the IRQs from the Control Panel | System | Device Manager | Network Adapters screen shown in Figure 16-4.

SETTING THE IRQ WITH SOFTWARE

There are two methods likely to be used in setting the IRQ with software. Either the NIC manufacturer will have supplied a software configuration program, or you may be able to use the computer's operating system software to set or adjust the IRQ. Figure 16-5 shows a 3Com network adapter card configuration program.

It sometimes is necessary to use both methods to set the IRQ, to be sure that the operating system and the NIC are agreed on which IRQ is to be used for the NIC. Sometimes the motherboard's BIOS/CMOS must also agree, or have a related setting disabled, for a software IRQ change to be effective.

Again, the safest procedure is to change only one tiny thing at a time, backtracking one step each time to be sure you have not lost ground or functionality. Testing IRQ changes can be very

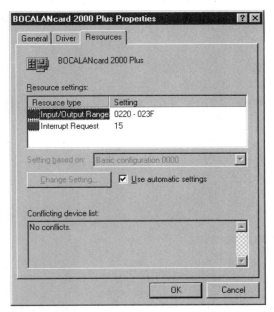

Fig. 16-4. IRQ information is available, and IRQs may be adjusted, on this screen.

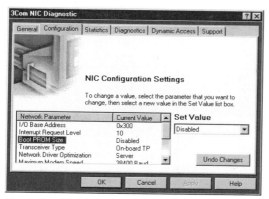

Fig. 16-5. This 3COM diagnostic and configuration program comes with the 3COM network adapter card.

time consuming, so taking notes on careful, methodical progress is probably a better use of your time than random trials without notes or planning.

Setting I/O Port Base Addresses

Like the IRQ, the I/O port base address that you assign to a network adapter card must be unique. No other device may also use that I/O port base address.

Refer to the documentation for your network adapter card and other hardware devices to find what I/O addresses are required or optional for your system.

Most devices in x86 computers have unique default I/O port base addresses. If an I/O port appears to be in conflict between two devices, the I/O port on one of the devices can usually be moved to another setting. Table 16-3 shows some common I/O port addresses. Use the same general procedure to resolve I/O port base address conflicts that you use to resolve IRQ conflicts. Keep the process as simple as possible, to avoid wasting time.

For Review

- Each device must have a unique IRQ.
- Each device must have an IRQ it is compatible with.

Table 16-3. Each NIC Must Have a Unique I/O Port Base Address.

I/O Port Address	Default Use
3F8	COM1
3BC	—
378	LPT1
300	—
2F8	COM2
278	LPT2

- IRQ3 may be available if COM2 has been disabled.
- IRQ5 may be available if the computer has no sound card and does not use LPT2.
- IRQ2 and IRQ9 are generally not available.
- Use the same methods to resolve I/O port base address conflicts that you use to resolve IRQ conflicts.

CHAPTER 17

Taming the Network

When Henry Ford built his first automobile, the idea was revolutionary, yet the effect of this new invention on most people was trivial—it was a novelty. At that time, no one knew the automobile would radically change our world in only a few short years. Today our lifestyles and occupations depend on automobile transportation. Likewise, back then no one could guess the amount of problems this new invention would cause. Traffic jams, pollution, fossil fuel consumption, accidents, and rising automobile expenses are serious issues experts seek solutions for every day.

Computer networking had much the same effect. At first, it was a novelty. A few computers could be connected with cable, allowing them to share resources. But in today's global marketplace, networking has become extremely complex and centrally important. Medium- to large-size companies run the risk of failure without effective and reliable networking capabilities—and the problems complex networks can experience are enough to make even the most adept network administrator's head spin.

For a network to be effective, it must be able to provide security, reliability, the services needed to the users, and it must be able to grow as the environment grows. To enable this, a network administrator must be able to quickly and effectively manage network

---

problems and keep network operation under control. This chapter explores some common network problems administrators face and the methods they use to control these problems.

Common Network Problems

Many problems may adversely affect network performance. Networks today are vast arrays of complex, expensive equipment. An administrator must carefully evaluate problems that arise and determine how to best cope with the problem or seek a practical solution. Let's explore some of the most common network problems administrators must face daily.

Attenuation

Attenuation refers to the degradation of signal as it travels along the cable. As a signal travels along a cable, it tends to weaken and become distorted. Corrupt packets that are unreadable by the receiving computer may result from attenuation. Different types of cable have different lengths that packets can travel before attenuation begins to occur, as shown in Table 17-1.

NOTE
Fiber-optic cable does not experience attenuation. Because fiber-optic networks send data by using modulated pulses of light and not an electronic signal, electrical attenuation is not an issue.

Fortunately, attenuation is often a simple problem to solve. A repeater can join cable segments that extend beyond the maximum allowed design length. A repeater is a device that regener-

Table 17-1. Each Cable Type Has Design Parameters to Prevent Attenuation.

Cable Type	Length to Attenuation
unshielded twisted pair	100 meters before attenuation
ThinNet	185 meters before attenuation
ThickNet	500 meters before attenuation

ates, grooms, and retimes the signal and sends it on to the next cable segment. Proper network planning and implementation can easily control attenuation.

Cable Failures

At the physical level, cable breaks can affect the network in a variety of ways. Depending on the network topology, a cable break may isolate a single computer so that it cannot gain access to network services. Or, a cable break may isolate an entire segment, including dozens of computers, printers, and other devices. In a bus topology, a trunk cable break can bring the network to a screeching halt, as shown in Figure 17-1.

In the example shown in Figure 17-1, the cable break on the main trunk stops all network activity. Because bus topologies require terminators to kill signal bounce, no computers on this network will be able to communicate with each other. The network no longer has proper termination, and cannot function.

In larger networks, a cable break is more likely to bring only a segment down. For example, in a star topology, a cable break on a segment could isolate the entire segment, as shown in Figure 17-2.

Cable breaks tend to be very different from environment to environment. One medium-size company may seldom experience a cable break while another medium-size company could be plagued by breaks. A number of factors cause cable breaks, such as the quality of the cable and installation, as well as changes being made to the environment. Facilities that are constantly under construction due to growth or changes within the organization are obviously more susceptible to cable failures than others.

Cable breaks and failures are often easy to repair, but may be difficult to isolate *in order to repair*. A number of tools are available to help isolate cable breaks. Many of these tools are discussed in Chapter 20, "Troubleshooting."

Fig. 17-1. A trunk break in a bus topology will bring down the network.

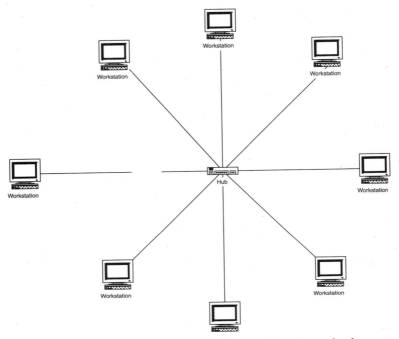

Fig. 17-2. A segment break in a star topology will isolate only the computer(s) on that segment.

Crosstalk

A related issue with cable quality and installation is crosstalk. Crosstalk refers to the "bleeding" or "overflow" of signal from one adjacent cable to another. This interference can be thought of as "noise" that corrupts the "good" signal on the other cable. Crosstalk can affect all types of cable, except fiber optic. UTP is especially susceptible to crosstalk—the shielding in STP provides protection from crosstalk and other interference.

Beaconing

On Token Ring and FDDI networks, beaconing is a process of computers signaling that token passing has been interrupted by a serious error and, through elimination, identifying where the error is likely to be. Beaconing is also discussed in Chapter 11, "Designing Your Network Architecture."

Bottlenecks

An issue related to packet collisions is a network "bottleneck." If a network device, such as a server or printer, cannot handle service requests during peak usage times, then a "bottleneck" occurs. While the overloaded device attempts to service requests, slow performance results and users wait, sometimes an unfortunate amount of time, for each service request to be fulfilled.

Think of a bottleneck like an entrance ramp on a freeway. If the ramp is too small to handle the number of cars accessing the freeway, the cars eventually "jam" and must wait to get on the freeway. A network bottleneck is the same. The solution to network bottlenecks is to upgrade the overloaded device so that it can handle the network load. This may involve more RAM, a faster CPU, additional CPUs, or even a new device. Windows NT Server provides a network monitoring tool that allows the administrator to find network bottlenecks so that they can be quickly corrected.

Broadcast Storms

A broadcast message is a packet that is sent to all nodes on the network. A broadcast storm occurs when there are more broadcast messages being sent onto the network than the network bandwidth can handle. The network becomes saturated with frames so that no frames get to their destinations. To continue our freeway traffic example, if more cars get on the freeway than the lanes can handle, a traffic jam or even gridlock occurs and the cars simply sit in place. A broadcast storm is similar, and broadcast storms can shut down a network.

Broadcast storms can be controlled by limiting the number of broadcasts made on the network. Some protocols, such as NetBEUI, use a broadcast method for communication and some access control methods do as well (see CSMA/CA—*think Appletalk,* for example, which is discussed later in the chapter). By using a protocol unlike NetBEUI, a network administrator can reduce broadcast traffic. Broadcast traffic can be further controlled by placing routers between segments because routers do not pass broadcast traffic to another segment. Network segment connection devices are described later in this chapter and in Chapter 12, "Network Topology Building Blocks."

Jabber

Jabber is a broad term for a network error caused by a network interface card improperly transmitting corrupt data or longer packets than allowed on the network. Because CSMA/CD network devices listen for inactivity to determine whether the network is available for transmission, a jabbering device can cause the network activity to halt because all devices think the network is busy.

Jitter

In a Token Ring or FDDI environment, a problem known as *jitter* may occur. Jitter refers to the instability of a signal wave on a token ring. Jitter is usually caused by some kind of signal interference or an unbalanced ring. This problem creates unreliable data delivery. Jitter can be solved by isolating the cause of the problem and eliminating that factor. If some device is causing interference, that device can be eliminated or upgraded. Remember that Token Ring represents a logical ring within the hub, although the actual topology is a star. Heavily populated segments and minimally populated segments may need to be "balanced" to avoid jitter.

The problems explained in this section are some of the more common ones network administrators must control to avoid network performance degradation. The next two sections explore some tips and tools that help solve or control these problems.

Packet Collisions

Only one packet may travel on a network cable at a time. At first glance, one packet at a time seems to be a very slow and cumbersome way for a whole network to communicate. However, because packets travel closer to the speed of light than the automobiles we referred to earlier, the speed of transmission is not an issue in ordinary 10-Mbps Ethernet. Packet collisions occur when two packets are placed on the cable at or *about the same time* and collide with each other. The collision mangles the data so that the data is unusable and the packets must be resent, as shown in Figure 17-3.

When two network nodes transmit at the same time, a *jam* is signaled and all devices stop transmission for a brief, random amount of time.

Packet collisions occur on networks that use a contention method of transmission, such as Ethernet networks. In this type

Fig. 17-3. Packet collision on the network cable.

of network, the computers "compete" or "contend" for the opportunity to send data over the network. Despite checking for an ongoing transmission before sending, collisions still occur.

Token Ring networks are not susceptible to collisions because the sending computer must always possess the token to send data—the rule that the sending computer must have a token to transmit, and the fact that there is only one token, forces each computer to take its turn. For more information about the differences between Ethernet and Token Ring transmission methods, refer to Chapter 11, "Designing Your Network Architecture," and Chapter 13, "Network Architecture on the Exam."

These two "access control methods" used to control network traffic and collisions are further discussed later in this chapter.

Generally speaking, network collisions do not adversely affect network performance and should be expected. If the *number* of collisions becomes high, say over 50 percent, this may slow the network and is usually a sign that there are too many nodes on a particular segment. At this point, the network administrator may decide to further segment the network to correct the problem. (See "Network Segmentation Devices" later in this chapter.)

Traffic Control Solutions

As you understand from the previous section, controlling network traffic is of utmost importance to keeping the network operating at a satisfactory speed. This section takes a look at the more common ways of controlling network traffic.

CSMA/CD and CSMA/CA

To make sure packets get delivered in a timely fashion and to avoid collisions, two access control methods are used in Ethernet. These methods are also known as *access methods*. Simply put, they are restraint mechanisms in place to control how computers send data. There is a set of rules and regulations that govern how we drive in automobile traffic. If there were no stop lights, no speed limits, and so forth, travel in populated areas would be impossible. The same ideas apply to the network environment. Computers have an access control method in an Ethernet environment to avoid "traffic jams" and collisions. The first is Carrier Sense Multiple Access with Collision Detection (CSMA/CD). With CSMA/CD, a computer "listens" to the cable to see if it is free. If no other computer is sending data, then the first computer sends data over the cable. This "listening" is accomplished by testing for a "carrier," which is a certain level of voltage. So the Carrier Sense Multiple Access component attempts to make certain that no two computers are putting data on the cable at the same time. Likewise, the computer also listens for collisions. If a collision occurs, the sending computers wait for a random period of time before resending the data. Thus, the Collision Detection component of CSMA/CD makes sure data is resent in the event of a collision.

The second type of access method is Carrier Sense Multiple Access with Collision Avoidance (CSMA/CA) and is often seen in AppleTalk environments. CSMA/CA is similar to CSMA/CD, except for the second component, Collision Avoidance. With this type of access method, each computer signals the other computers of its intent to send data, thus "avoiding" collisions. CSMA/CA is not as popular as CSMA/CD because of the amount of broadcast traffic. With each computer broadcasting its intent to send data, network traffic is greatly increased, even though it is doing this to avoid collisions.

Token Passing

Token Ring environments have a built-in collision control method. Because each computer must possess the token to send data, two computers cannot put data on the cable at the same time. Token passing and token-ring environments are discussed in more detail in Chapter 11, "Designing Your Network Architecture," and Chapter 13, "Network Architecture on the Exam."

Network Segmentation Devices

Network traffic problems are normally caused due to overcrowding of network segments. Thus, devices that can further segment the network greatly reduce traffic problems and other network issues. The following devices each provide different services for the network, and a more detailed discussion of each device can be found in Chapter 12, "Network Topology Building Blocks."

Bridge

A network bridge is a device that can join two LANs or two segments. Bridges are primarily used to increase the length of a segment or the number of nodes for a network. Bridges function at the data link layer of the OSI reference model.

Router

A router is a device used to connect networks of different types. In other words, a router can connect two networks using different architectures. Routers determine the best route to get a packet to its destination, but a router will not pass broadcast traffic, which is a great advantage in many network situations. Routers function at the network layer of the OSI reference model.

Brouter

A brouter combines the best features of a bridge and a router. A brouter can act as a bridge for networks that are alike and a router for networks that are different. Brouters function at both the data link layer and network layer of the OSI reference model.

Gateway

A network gateway is powerful software and/or hardware that links two networks using different protocols. Gateways function at the network layer of the OSI reference model.

TIP

It is important for the test that you know which layers of the OSI reference model bridges, routers, brouters, and gateways function at. Expect several questions on this issue alone! Although gateways exist that are said to function at all levels of the OSI reference model, the exam expects you to know that gateways generally operate from the network layer on up through the application layer. Table 17-2 summarizes the OSI reference model layers for these four devices.

Table 17-2. Segmentation Devices Work at Various Layers of the OSI Reference Model.

Device	OSI Reference Model Layer
gateway	application through network layers (7, 6, 5, 4, 3)
brouter	network and data link layers (3 & 2)
router	network layer (3)
bridge	data link layer (2)

For Review

- Network administrators must control network traffic and performance issues. Cable breaks, crosstalk, attenuation, bottlenecks, collisions, and jitter are some of the more common network traffic problems.

- Network traffic and performance problems can be controlled through both hardware and software solutions. CSMA/CD and CSMA/CA are access methods to control how computers put data on the cable in Ethernet environments. Token Ring environments use token passing to avoid packet collisions.

- Segmentation devices such as bridges, routers, brouters, and gateways allow connecting segments or LANs together.

CHAPTER 18

Node Addressing

Imagine this scenario: You work in a corporate environment that employs over five thousand people. You depend on resources and information from a large number of fellow employees. Now imagine each person in this environment does not have a name, including yourself. In fact, no one even has a social security number, credit card, driver's license, or any other form of identification. The task of contacting and working with each person would become more than difficult. In fact, the simple concept of "names" makes effective communication among humans possible—more than we even realize.

The same is true with computers. For communication to take place among networked computers, there must be a way for computers to identify each other as unique machines with unique resources to offer. This concept is referred to as *node addressing*.

At its most basic level, a network node refers to any device on the network capable of communicating with other nodes. Clients, servers, repeaters, bridges, and so forth are all considered network nodes. Each node must have a unique name and number or "address" so that other nodes can communicate with it.

The concept of node addressing often appears simple at first glance, yet this concept is one that often causes confusion among

MCSE candidates because of a failure to understand how node addressing concepts and terminology integrate with each other. This chapter examines several methods of node addressing, the differences between them, and how the various methods of node addressing integrate on a network.

OSI Reference Model

To begin our discussion of node addressing, we must first return to the OSI reference model in Chapter 9. Hopefully, you have memorized the reference model now and understand the tasks that are performed at each layer. The important aspect to remember for node addressing is the fact that the OSI reference model represents virtual communication from one computer to another.

When first learning the OSI reference model, we often memorize the model from top to bottom, but you have to remember that the model represents the communication between two computers and what happens at each layer in the communication process. The key to comprehending node addressing is to constantly remember that the application layer of one computer corresponds to *and communicates with* the application layer of another computer, that the presentation layer of one computer corresponds to *and communicates with* the presentation layer of another computer, and so forth.

Think of it this way: Pretend there is a seven-story building with one person on each floor. A clipboard with paperwork is passed from floor to floor through a small hole in the ceiling. Each person has a specific task to complete with the paperwork, and does not know what the people on the other floors are doing with the paperwork and doesn't even care.

Across the street, another seven-story building with a person on each floor is doing the same thing. The top floor of building A is aware of what is going on at the top floor of building B, but is not aware of the other floors and the work being performed in its own building or the building across the street—the OSI layers are the same. Each layer has specific purposes and tasks within the communication process and is unaware of what goes on in the neighboring layer. It understands primarily what is going on at the same layer on another computer. With that said, let's begin looking at the concepts of node addressing and relating the concepts to the OSI reference model.

NetBIOS

NetBIOS stands for *Network Basic Input/Output System*. It is the basic network connectivity service provided by Windows NT. Net-BIOS is not a protocol—it is an application programming inter-face (API) that allows the computer to participate in and use network services. The NetBIOS architecture is the basis of node addressing for Microsoft networking components. NetBIOS names identify computers on the network, accomplished by a unique naming system. NetBIOS names can be up to 15 charac-ters in length, and *cannot* contain

"/ \ * , . " @"

or any blank spaces. In addition to the 15-character name, a six-teenth invisible character is used to identify the kind of service being offered by the computer, such as the server or workstation service, or even identification as a domain controller. When a Net-BIOS name is less than 15 characters in length, NetBIOS "pads" the other characters with blanks to reach the sixteenth character. So, a NetBIOS name can be up to 15 characters in length, with the six-teenth character reserved, and must be unique on the network.

The NetBIOS name is often what we consider to be the "friendly name" of the computer, such as Computer12, Corpo-rate1, or even the user's first name. Any name can apply, as long as it is unique on the network and conforms to the standards above. NetBIOS names make it easy for the users to identify which computer is which.

Typical NetBIOS Computer Names

Research1	Corporate1
Research32	SGServer6
ResearchServ1	Mary
Sales1	Billiesmac
MarketingServ1	Albert

NetBIOS is considered a session level interface (OSI reference model level 5, counting from the physical, bottom layer). Net-BIOS enables computers to establish a communication "session" between two or more network devices. Figure 18-1 illustrates the

Computer1   **Computer2**

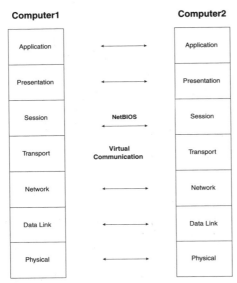

Application	←———→	Application
Presentation	←———→	Presentation
Session	**NetBIOS** ←——	Session
Transport	**Virtual Communication**	Transport
Network	←———→	Network
Data Link	←———→	Data Link
Physical	←———→	Physical

Fig. 18-1. Each layer of Computer1 communicates with the corresponding layer of other computers.

concept that Computer1 communicates with corresponding layers of Computer2.

Once this session is established, the devices may begin communicating with each other. However, for a session to be set up, each node must establish itself as a unique entity on the network—in other words, each computer must have a node name that is unique on the network.

In a NetBIOS network, name resolution is broadcast based. When a computer boots, a name registration request is broadcast on the local network. If no objections to the name are made, then the computer may use the name on the network. If the name is already in use, the node previously holding the name will protest by issuing a negative name registration response datagram, and the requesting computer will not be able to use that name on the network. In other words, if two computers have the NetBIOS name of "computer6," only the first computer to log onto the network will be able to use this name. The second "computer6" will be issued a negative name registration datagram by the first computer when it attempts to register a duplicate name on the network. The second computer will not be allowed to participate on the network until the first "computer6" logs off or one of the two computers undergoes a name change.

TIP

You can change a computer's name by right clicking Network Neighborhood, selecting Properties, and using the Identification tab to make the change. The NetBIOS name of a networked computer may also be viewed at the Windows NT command prompt by entering "nbtstat -n."

NOTE

Because NetBIOS name resolution uses the broadcast method, larger networks may experience too much NetBIOS broadcast traffic. NetBIOS is most effective in small-to-medium LAN environments.

So, the session layer of the OSI reference model understands NetBIOS names and can communicate with the corresponding layers of other computers by addressing their NetBIOS names on the network.

In regard to NetBIOS, an important responsibility the network administrator faces is the implementation of a logical, well-planned NetBIOS naming scheme for the network. There are no hard and fast rules for this implementation, but the following points should be carefully considered:

- The NetBIOS naming scheme should logically organize the network.

- The NetBIOS naming scheme should enable the users to clearly identify computers, servers, and resources available.

- The NetBIOS naming scheme should be flexible enough to easily allow for changes and additions to the network.

A number of naming combinations are available, depending on the needs of the users and network administrators. The naming scheme may even be different within various departments. Consider the examples shown in Tables 18-1 and 18-2.

As you can see in the examples, the two departments' naming schemes vary in that one uses a name and number scheme while the other focuses on server names and user names. Both are effective naming conventions—the point is that the network naming scheme should follow a logical organization and stick to that particular organization. An effective naming scheme makes the network easier to administer and enables the users to quickly locate needed resources.

Table 18-1.
Accounting Department NetBIOS Naming Scheme.*

Corpserver1	corporate primary domain controller
Corpserver2	corporate backup domain controller
AcctAppServ1	accounting applications server
AcctFileServ1	accounting file server
AcctPrint1	accounting laser jet
Workstation1	user workstation
Workstation2	user workstation
Workstation3	user workstation
Workstation4	user workstation

* Accounting's NetBIOS naming scheme is based on names and numbers.

Table 18-2.
Marketing Department NetBIOS Naming Scheme.*

Corpserver1	corporate primary domain controller
Corpserver2	corporate backup domain controller
MktApps	marketing applications server
MktFiles	marketing file server
MktPrinter	marketing laser jet
lsmith	user workstation
kwillis	user workstation
mmontgomery	user workstation
sreed	user workstation

* Marketing's NetBIOS naming scheme is based on names.

Universal Naming Convention—UNC

An issue that sometimes causes confusion in relation to NetBIOS names is the use of UNC—*Universal Naming Convention* names. The UNC is simply a way to access a shared resource on a computer that already has a NetBIOS name. Think of the Universal Naming Convention as a postal address. A postal address always consists of a name and some kind of location information, such as a street address, city, state, and zip code. This is a uniform method for sending mail from one person to another. The UNC name is the same. It provides a uniform method for accessing computers and named shares located on those computers. So, the NetBIOS name is the actual name of the computer and the UNC is simply a way to get to that computer. The UNC name is represented in the following manner:

```
\\computername\sharename
```

The UNC consists of the computer name and share name and is accessed via the Run command in Windows NT and Windows 95/98. The UNC always begins with two backslashes and the computer's NetBIOS name:

```
\\computer6
```

In a NetBIOS network, entering \\computer6 at the command prompt would provide the user with a list of all the resources that are shared and available on computer6. The command can be further refined if the user knows the name of a shared resource he or she would like to access. This increased specificity is accomplished by an additional backslash and the name of the shared folder or resource:

```
\\computer6\docs
```

In the above example, the folder "docs" is a shared resource on computer6. If the name of the actual document the user would like to access is known, the UNC can be further refined with an additional backslash and the name of the shared document:

```
\\computer6\docs\keynote.ppt
```

The shared PowerPoint presentation, keynote.ppt, may then be accessed directly by using the UNC name. UNC names allow quick access to network resources, especially familiar resources that are often used.

Of course, the UNC is only one way to access a computer and its share(s). Access to resources may also be accomplished through a GUI by using Network Neighborhood on Windows 95/98 and Windows NT machines.

Transmission Control Protocol/Internet Protocol (TCP/IP)

TCP/IP stands for Transmission Control Protocol/Internet Protocol. This suite of protocols is the communication standard on the Internet. Because TCP/IP has become so popular during the past several years, many LAN environments today use TCP/IP to ensure compatibility with the Internet. TCP/IP addressing is represented by four "octets," such as 131.107.2.200, with the first one to three octets representing the network, and the last two or three octets representing the host machine. It is beyond the scope of this book and the Networking Essentials exam to provide a full discussion of IP addressing, but you do need to understand where IP falls into the node addressing scheme.

Humans are language-based creatures. No matter how great our math skills, our brains function on a language basis. Computers, however, communicate through mathematical numbers, specifically binary math. Bridging this gap between humans and computers requires the conversion of NetBIOS names to mathematical addresses. So, NetBIOS names, though useful to us, must be translated to be mathematically based. This is accomplished at the transport and network layers of the OSI reference model, as shown in Figure 18-2.

There are several systems available on a Windows NT network to resolve the NetBIOS names to IP addresses so that communication may continue on a network. These systems are not technically a part of the node addressing process or the OSI reference model, but you should have a general understanding of the systems used to resolve names to IP addresses for the test. The Networking Essentials exam does not focus on these, but you should at least be familiar with them so that their use on the exam does not confuse you.

NetBIOS name cache. This local cache contains the local computer NetBIOS name and the IP addresses of computers that have recently been resolved.

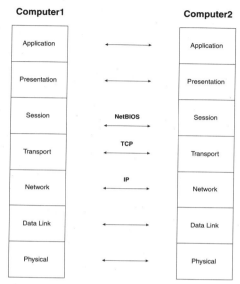

Computer1

Computer2

Application		Application
Presentation		Presentation
Session	NetBIOS	Session
Transport	TCP	Transport
Network	IP	Network
Data Link		Data Link
Physical		Physical

Fig. 18-2. TCP operates at the transport layer, and IP operates at the network layer of the OSI reference model.

Windows Internet Naming Service (WINS). This service provides resolution of NetBIOS names to IP addresses. WINS is a server service that provides dynamic mapping of NetBIOS computer names to IP addresses. Most networks that use WINS also use DHCP, or Dynamic Hosts Configuration Protocol. Because the task of manually assigning each node a four-octet IP address in a large network would require great administrative overhead and the potential for errors and duplicate IP addresses, a DHCP server often takes care of this need by "leasing" an IP address to a node and making certain that no duplicate IP addresses are provided. In short, a node's IP address may not remain the same, so the WINS server is used to resolve the NetBIOS name to the current four-octet IP addresses.

NetBIOS Broadcast. A broadcast packet is sent over the network requesting the resolution of a particular NetBIOS name. A computer that can resolve the NetBIOS name can answer the broadcast and help the broadcasting computer resolve the NetBIOS name to an IP address.

LMHOSTS file. This is a text file located on the local machine that maps the NetBIOS name to the IP address. LMHOSTS files are static files that must be manually updated, but they still provide necessary service in some networking circumstances. LMHOSTS files are useful in very small networks where each computer's four-octet IP address does not change frequently (as it would in a larger network using DHCP) or to provide a name and address map to servers or other network devices that have permanent IP addresses.

HOSTS file. This is a static text file located on the local machine that maps hosts' names to IP addresses. HOSTS files reflect the same concept as LMHOSTS except the static HOSTS file is designed to map a computer's host name, such as *www.microsoft .com* to an IP address.

Typical Host Names

www.3com.com

marketing.foobar.net

violet.flowering.org

Example HOSTS File

127.0.0.1	localhost	
10.0.1.21	server2	#BDC
10.0.1.60	server1	#PDC
199.170.88.90	mx2.io.com	#Outgoing E-mail
199.170.88.29	illuminati.io.com	#IO DNS Server
199.170.88.10	illuminati.io.com	#IO DNS Server
206.224.86.3	as3.wc-aus.io.com	
199.170.88.1	aus-gw-F0-0.illuminati.net	
199.170.88.5	pentagon.io.com	
199.170.88.6	xanadu.io.com	
199.170.88.7	bermuda.io.com	
199.170.88.8	atlantis.io.com	

Domain Name System (DNS). A DNS server holds a database that maps host names to IP addresses. DNS is similar to WINS in that it resolves names, but instead of a computer NetBIOS name, DNS resolves a host name to an IP address. DNS is responsible for resolving Internet names, called *Fully Qualified Domain Names* (FQDN). For example, *www.microsoft.com* is a FQDN, consisting of the site name and "com," the domain, which is short for "commercial." Other domain extensions in use are "int" for NATO and international organizations, "org" for organization, "net" for Internet services, "mil" for military, "gov" for government, and "edu" for post-secondary education. As with NetBIOS, fully qualified domain names make navigating the Internet easy for the user. For example www.sfasu.edu is resolved to the IP address of 144.96.210.215. It is much easier for the user to remember "sfasu.edu" than 144.96.210.215.

Each Internet name equals an IP address and the computer, through either a static HOSTS file or DNS, must resolve the name to the IP address to reach the site. For example:

- www.realtorads.com = 38.248.210.75
- world.std.com = 192.74.137.5
- moe.rice.edu = 128.42.5.4

If you use Internet Explorer or Netscape Navigator, you can see the FQDN being resolved at the bottom left side of your browser when you type in the URL—if you look quickly. If you type http://www.sfasu.edu you will see at the bottom left of the browser "Looking for sfasu.edu," then after the name is resolved it will say "connecting to 144.96.210.215" for a brief moment.

MAC Address

Once a NetBIOS name is resolved to an IP address, the resolution must be taken down to a lower level on the OSI reference model— the data link layer. Remember that the data link layer is made up of two sublayers, the media access control sublayer and the logical link control sublayer. A computer's MAC Address (*Media Access Control*) is a hard-coded unique address found on the computer's NIC card. Because the address is hard-coded, it never changes. The user is able to change the NetBIOS name and even the IP address if desired, but the MAC address remains constant unless the computer is given a new NIC card.

Remember that the OSI reference model represents virtual communication between two computers. The data link layer (layer two) is concerned with addressing at the data link layer on the NIC card and subsequent data link layer addressing on another machine, as shown in Figure 18-3.

The Global View

Now that we have examined the major concepts of node addressing, let's look at an example in Figure 18-4. On a network, Computer14 needs a resource available on Computer12.

To access this resource, Computer14 seeks to establish a session with Computer12. This is accomplished through virtual communication in the OSI model, but in reality takes place by Computer14 sending Computer12 a packet.

Next, the NetBIOS names must be resolved for the computers to communicate on the network. Computer14 resolves its own IP address and the IP address of Computer12. This is done through any means available, such as the NetBIOS name cache, WINS, LMHOSTS file, or other methods.

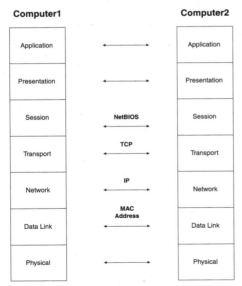

Fig. 18-3. Media Access Control (MAC) addresses operate at the data link layer.

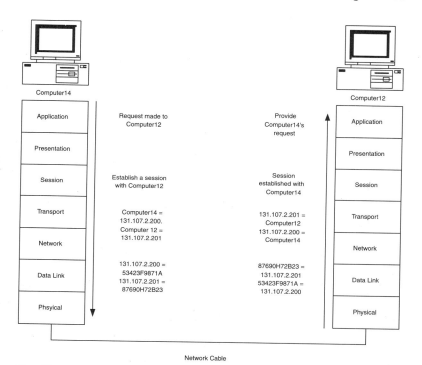

Fig. 18-4. One half of a communication cycle using the OSI reference model.

Once the NetBIOS names are resolved to IP addresses, the IP addresses are then resolved to the MAC addresses for network communication. The packet is then sent over the network to Computer12 and the process is reversed.

From the received packet, Computer12 begins resolving Computer14's MAC address, IP address, and finally the NetBIOS name and data request. The session is officially established at this point and Computer12 may fulfill the request made by Computer14.

This example shows a model of how node addressing functions in Microsoft networking. We should note, however, the OSI reference model is a standard for communication on *all* networks. Other networking environments follow the same basic model.

For example, the Novell NetWare environment uses a different computer naming scheme than NetBIOS at the session layer. Yet, protocol addressing with IPX/SPX still occurs at the transport and network layers while the NIC card still uses a hard-coded address.

The major point the MCSE candidate must remember is that node addressing encompasses several addressing methods that all work together through the OSI reference model. The NetBIOS naming convention should be seen as a part of the whole and not an entity in and of itself.

Use Table 18-3 as a study guide for node addressing.

For Review

- The OSI model represents virtual communication between two computers. Each layer has its own tasks and responsibilities, understands, and corresponds with the same layer on another computer.

- NetBIOS is a method to assign "friendly" names for computers. Each computer on the network must have a unique NetBIOS name. NetBIOS functions at the session layer of the OSI reference model.

- Friendly names must be converted to numerical addressing for

Table 18-3. NetBIOS, IP, and MAC Addresses Each Have a Role in Node Addressing.

NetBIOS names	Allows friendly computer names on the network. "Computer7" and similar names are all NetBIOS and can be configured by the user. NetBIOS works at the session layer of the OSI reference model.
IP addresses	NetBIOS names must be resolved to IP addresses for network communication to occur. Resolution may be accomplished through WINS, LMHOSTS, local name cache, and other methods. TCP functions at the transport layer and IP functions at the network layer of the OSI reference model.
MAC addresses	The IP address must be resolved to a hard-coded MAC address found on the NIC card. MAC addresses function at the data link layer of the OSI reference model.

network communication to occur. This occurs at the transport and network layers where network protocols reside. Several systems, such as WINS, HOSTS, LMHOSTS, and DNS provide computer name and host name resolution.

■ IP addresses are resolved to MAC addresses. MAC addresses are hard-coded numerical addresses on the NIC card. The MAC addresses reside at the data link layer of the OSI reference model.

PART FIVE

Keeping It All Running

This section covers several topics essential to network design and operation. Network Administrators and network support staff perform network monitoring and troubleshooting tasks everyday. Network designers must plan for disaster recovery and fault tolerance to preserve the investment in the network, and to preserve the integrity of the network.

Chapter 19, "Network Monitoring," covers creating a performance baseline database for the network and dealing with bottlenecks using Performance Monitor, network monitors, and Protocol Analyzers.

Chapter 20, "Troubleshooting," explains several network diagnostic tools including digital volt meters, time domain reflectometers, oscilloscopes, advanced cable testers, and protocol analyzers. This chapter also covers Windows NT TCP/IP utilities and general troubleshooting principles.

Chapter 21, "Disaster Recovery," covers risk assessment, gathering contingent resources, redundancy, and backup.

Chapter 22, "Fault Tolerance," includes uninterruptable power supplies, topology, RAID disk management, and Windows NT Disk Administrator.

CHAPTER 19

Network Monitoring

Creating a baseline for your network is an important step in maintaining a healthy network. A baseline establishes the performance of the network under normal operating conditions. Baseline measurements should be taken for over a period of a week or longer. As part of the monitoring process, future network operations can be compared to the baseline. These comparisons can be analyzed to review resource usage to:

- Record typical network usage.
- Plan for future growth of the network.
- Isolate bottlenecks causing a decrease in network performance.

A bottleneck is the step or resource using the most time of a larger operation and constricting the workflow of the network. Bottlenecks can occur due to many conditions, including:

- Inefficient use of resources
- Resource speed
- Resource capacity

Three tools useful in creating a network baseline and monitoring the network are:

- Performance Monitor
- Network monitors
- Protocol Analyzers

Performance Monitor

Windows NT built-in Performance Monitor provides a network administrator with a graphical tool to collect data regularly throughout each day so trends can be determined through analysis of the data. By monitoring the network, an administrator knows whether a network needs more memory here, a faster hard disk drive there, or a new processor in another place.

Performance Monitor can be found on Windows NT Workstation and Windows NT Server in the Administrative Tools program group. Data from Performance Monitor can be viewed in real time, logged for future comparisons, and easily used in charts and reports. The log files can also be exported for further analysis in other applications, such as Microsoft Excel or Microsoft Access. Alerts can be set to warn the administrator when threshold values have been exceeded.

Performance Monitor collects data about system resources, called *objects,* and statistical information, called *counters.*

A few of the objects available for monitoring are:

Cache	Process
LogicalDisk	Processor
Memory	Redirector
Objects	System
Paging file	Thread
PhysicalDisk	

Each object in Performance Monitor has many subcategories containing counters. A specific set of counters for an object can be selected depending on your monitoring needs. For a specific counter definition, open the Add to Chart dialog box, select (highlight) the counter, and click on the Explain button.

Although additional resources (objects) can also be monitored, data on the following four object resources should be included in a network baseline:

- Memory
- Processor
- Hard disk drives
- Network

Memory

 To find.out if the computer needs additional RAM, set Performance Monitor to log data on

Object: memory   Counter: pages/sec

If the computer maintains a high rate of hard page faults, there is a memory bottleneck. Hard page faults occur when a program cannot find the data in memory (RAM) and must retrieve the data from the hard disk drive. If the computer has over five hard page faults a second for an extended time, additional RAM should be installed.

To obtain more information about the computer's memory use, log data on:

Object: memory   Counter: available bytes

Object: memory   Counter: committed bytes

Object: memory   Counter: pool nonpaged bytes

Figure 19-1 shows an example of a Performance Monitor chart with the above four counters.

Processor

 One way to monitor a CPU is to log data from:

Object: processor   Counter: % processor time

Processor: % Processor Time monitors the amount of time the CPU is in use. If the CPU operates over 75 percent processor time for extended periods, a faster processor or additional processors may be required.

For more information about CPU activity the following counters can be logged:

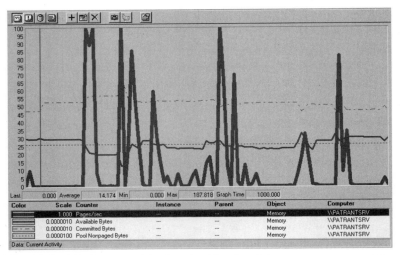

Fig. 19-1. A Performance Monitor chart logging data on memory resources.

Object: processor	Counter: % privileged time
Object: processor	Counter: % user time
Object: processor	Counter: interrupts/sec
Object: system	Counter: processor queue length
Object: server work queues	Counter: queue length

Figure 19-2 shows an example of a Performance Monitor chart with counters monitoring processor usage.

Hard Disk Drives

Performance Monitor (perfmon at the command prompt) can also log data for both PhysicalDisk and LogicalDisk objects. Physical-Disk can monitor the hard disk drive(s) for troubleshooting and capacity planning. LogicalDisk monitors the logical partitions on the hard disk drive(s). By finding the partition that is generating the disk activity, the network Administrator can track down an application that is generating excessive requests.

Because Performance Monitor disk counters can reduce performance by increasing disk access time approximately 1.5 percent on older x86 computers, disk counters are not automatically started in perfmon. Disk counters must be started manually by typing

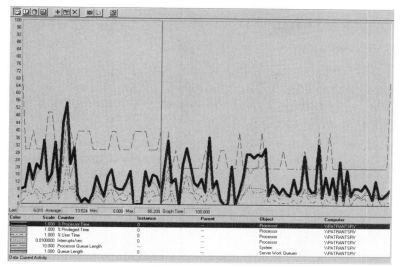

Fig. 19-2. A Performance Monitor chart logging data on processor resources.

```
Diskperf -y
```

at a command prompt. You will receive the following message:

```
Disk performance counters on this system are now set
to start at boot. This change will take effect after the
system is restarted.
```

Once the system has been restarted, the disk counters in Performance Monitor can be started.

 PhysicalDisk: % Disk Time charts the amount of time a hard disk drive uses to process read and write requests. If % Disk Time remains close to 100 percent, a faster controller, faster hard disk drives, or more hard drives in a RAID environment are indicated, assuming the computer has adequate RAM. See Chapter 22, "Fault Tolerance," for information on RAID.

Object: PhysicalDisk   Counter: % disk time

Other objects and counters to monitor for disk usage are:

Object: PhysicalDisk   Counter: avg. disk bytes/transfer

Object: PhysicalDisk   Counter: disk bytes/sec

Object: LogicalDisk   Counter: % free space

Figure 19-3 shows an example of a chart with counters monitoring hard disk drives.

Network

To determine the number of bytes the server is sending and receiving over the network, monitor the following:

Object: server   Counter: bytes total/sec

If this number is high, an additional network adapter card may be needed or the network may benefit from segmentation.

Other objects and counters to monitor in gathering data on your network are:

Object: network interface   Counter: bytes sent/sec

Object: network interface   Counter: bytes total/sec

To use the Performance Monitor counters for Network Interface, TCP/IP, Internet Control Message Protocol and UDP, the Simple Network Management Protocol (SNMP) service and the TCP/IP network protocol must be installed on the

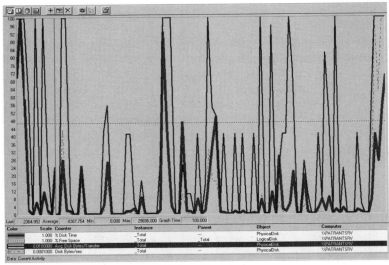

Fig. 19-3. A Performance Monitor chart logging data on disk resources.

computer you will be monitoring. SNMP is not automatically installed when TCP/IP is installed. To install SNMP, open Control Panel, choose the Network Icon, select the Services menu, and select the SNMP service, and click on Add.

NETWORK MONITORS

Network monitors are software programs that capture packets and provide information about the traffic sent and received by a computer on the network. The captured data can be reviewed on a packet-by-packet basis. Network monitor filters can be set so that only the packets of interest are saved. On the Networking Essentials examination, any mention of *network monitors* is likely to be a distracter—read the question carefully to decide if performance monitor or protocol analyzer wouldn't be a better answer.

Protocol Analyzers

 A Protocol Analyzer captures, filters, and analyzes traffic on the network. Protocol Analyzers are a combination of hardware and software products. A Protocol Analyzer can:

■ Capture, display, and filter packets directly from the network based on specified criteria, including protocols.

■ Monitor traffic on the network on a packet basis.

■ Monitor network bandwidth.

■ Analyze data to track network performance.

For Review

■ Use the Memory: Pages/sec counter in Performance Monitor to see if the computer needs additional RAM.

■ Use Processor: % Processor Time in Performance Monitor to track the percentage of time the CPU is in use.

■ Monitor PhysicalDisk: % Disk Time for disk usage information.

■ To monitor traffic on the network use the Server: Bytes Total/ sec counter.

■ The Simple Network Management Protocol (SNMP) service must be installed before the TCP/IP counters can be used in Performance Monitor.

■ Protocol Analyzers can

Capture packets directly from the network.

Monitor network traffic at the packet level.

Monitor network bandwidth.

From Here

See Chapter 22, "Fault Tolerance," for information on RAID. Chapter 20, "Troubleshooting," has further information on solving network problems.

CHAPTER 20

Troubleshooting

Troubleshooting Diagnostic Tools

There are several tools available to help identify hardware problems on the network. These tools save time and money by helping the network administrator to quickly find the location of the problem.

Digital Volt Meter (DVM)

A DVMs, also known as a *volt-ohm meter* (VOM) or multimeter, is a basic tool used to test electronic signals.

 DVMs are useful in networking environments because they can be used to determine if cable has a break that will halt network traffic. DVMs can reveal if two parts of the same cable are exposed and touching or if a broken part of the cable is touching another conductor.

Time Domain Reflectometer (TDR)

TDRs send sonarlike pulses along cable looking for breaks, shorts, crimps, or imperfections in a cable. TDRs look for these problems and provide a report to the administrator. Most TDRs can locate a cable break within a few feet of the actual fault or separation in the cable.

Oscilloscope

An oscilloscope is an instrument that measures the amount of signal voltage passing per unit of time. The results are displayed on a monitor, and this tool is useful to check network traffic speed and performance. Oscilloscopes can display shorts, crimps, breaks, and attenuation in cable.

Advanced Cable Testers

Advanced cable testers are sophisticated devices that work beyond the physical layer of the OSI reference model into the data link, network, and even transport layers. Advanced cable testers report on the physical condition of the cable and can also report frame counts, collisions, error frame counts, and even beaconing.

 Advanced cable testers are used to monitor the overall performance of the network and are able to report problems with a particular cable or NIC card.

Protocol Analyzers

Like advanced cable testers, Protocol Analyzers are sophisticated devices that work in the upper layers of the OSI reference model. Protocol Analyzers work in "real time," meaning they can analyze for the network administrator exactly what is going on concerning network traffic at the current moment. Most Protocol Analyzers have a built-in TDR and can capture and decode network packets to look inside the packet and identify the causes of network problems.

Protocol Analyzers are the primary tool covered on the exam that allows you to inspect inside packets. It is important for network administrators to be able to think of network communications at the packet level. For instance, a typical exam question expects you to eliminate a distracter answer by knowing that if you could somehow decrease the overall packet size on the network, network performance would almost certainly not be helped. The network is actually in worse shape with smaller packets, because it will require more packets to carry the same traffic, and more packets, in turn, mean more congestion and more overhead communication, etc. Larger packet sizes could conceivably help, but smaller packets won't.

Protocol Analyzers are used to identify network problems including connection errors, bottlenecks, traffic problems, and protocol problems.

 Protocol Analyzers can also generate statistics on network performance to help the administrator monitor and document problem areas. If you wanted to measure the effective bandwidth of your network, you would do it with a Protocol Analyzer.

 Of all these devices, the Protocol Analyzer is the only device that can decode and read network packets.

TIP

One Networking Essentials braindump on the Internet says that, *if a Protocol Analyzer is offered as an available answer,* then Protocol Analyzer is always the correct answer. This spurious advice is contradicted in another credible braindump. The grain of truth behind the matter is that *Protocol Analyzers* are definitely covered on the exam in multiple questions, and *Protocol Analyzer* is a correct answer on one or more questions.

TCP/IP Utilities

Because most networks today are moving to TCP/IP, we should mention a few of the Microsoft Windows 95/98/NT and TCP/IP utilities available to help both the administrator and the user identify connectivity problems. You will not be tested specifically on these utilities on the Networking Essentials exam, but you should be familiar with them to avoid confusion if they are used in an exam scenario.

Ping

Ping is a command to test connectivity to a specific computer, server, or router. To use the ping utility, go to the command prompt and type "ping" followed by the NetBIOS name (if WINS is enabled) or the IP address of the machine you wish to reach. If the ping is successful, you will get a reply as shown in Figure 20-1.

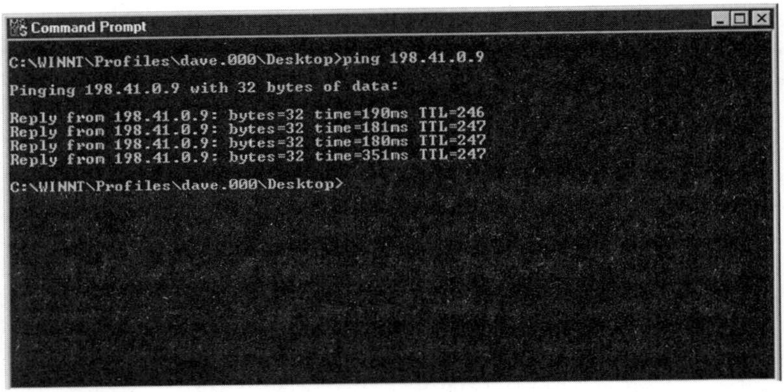

```
Command Prompt                                          _ □ ×

C:\WINNT\Profiles\dave.000\Desktop>ping 198.41.0.9

Pinging 198.41.0.9 with 32 bytes of data:

Reply from 198.41.0.9: bytes=32 time=190ms TTL=246
Reply from 198.41.0.9: bytes=32 time=181ms TTL=247
Reply from 198.41.0.9: bytes=32 time=180ms TTL=247
Reply from 198.41.0.9: bytes=32 time=351ms TTL=247

C:\WINNT\Profiles\dave.000\Desktop>
```

Fig. 20-1. Ping tells you whether your computer can communicate with a remote computer.

If the ping is not successful, you will get a reply as shown in the following

```
C:\WIN95\Desktop>ping 131.107.2.1

Pinging 131.107.2.1 with 32 bytes of data:

Request timed out.
Request timed out.
Request timed out.
Request timed out.
```

If you suspect there may be a connectivity problem with a particular computer, you can ping that computer using a built-in "self-test." The loopback self-test function is an IP address, 127.0.0.1, reserved for self-tests. This will test the NIC card to make sure it is functioning properly and is properly connected to the computer. A simple self-test ping also assures you that TCP/IP is installed and working on the computer. The following is an example of a successful self-test ping.

```
C:\WIN95\Desktop>ping 127.0.0.1

Pinging 127.0.0.1 with 32 bytes of data:

Reply from 127.0.0.1: bytes=32 time=1ms TTL=32
Reply from 127.0.0.1: bytes=32 time<10ms TTL=32
```

```
Reply from 127.0.0.1: bytes=32 time=1ms TTL=32
Reply from 127.0.0.1: bytes=32 time<10ms TTL=32

C:\WIN95\Desktop>
```

IPCONFIG

IPCONFIG is a utility that provides a variety of information about the computer's TCP/IP properties. The IPCONFIG command will identify the current IP address, subnet mask, and gateway address the computer is using. At the command prompt type:

```
ipconfig /all
```

to obtain the most complete report. Figure 20-2 is a sample of the output of the IPCONFIG command.

Netstat

Netstat displays protocol statistics and current TCP/IP connections for a particular computer. You can view the netstat options by typing

```
netstat /?
```

at the command prompt as shown here:

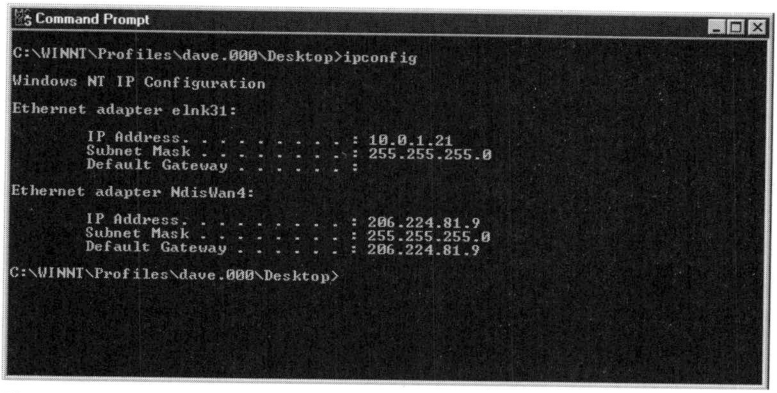

Fig. 20-2. IPCONFIG provides the IP address, subnet mask, and other information.

```
C:\WIN95\Desktop>netstat /?

NETSTAT[-a][-e][-n][-s][-p proto][-r][interval]
```

-a   Displays all connections and listening ports.
      (Server-side connections are normally not shown).
-e   Displays Ethernet statistics. This may be combined
      with the -s option.
-n   Displays addresses and port numbers in numerical
      form.
-p   proto Shows connections for the protocol
      specified by proto; proto may be tcp or udp. If
      used with the -s option to display per-protocol
      statistics, proto may be tcp, udp, or ip.
-r   Displays the contents of the routing table.
-s   Displays per-protocol statistics. By default,
      statistics are shown for TCP, UDP and IP; the
      -p option may be used to specify a subset of the
      default.
interval Redisplays selected statistics, pausing
      interval seconds between each display. Press
      CTRL+C to stop redisplaying statistics. If
      omitted, netstat will print the current con-
      figuration information once.

Tracert

Tracert is a utility that allows you to trace the route, or number of hops from one computer to another. Tracert is useful to see how packets are routed in a LAN environment and can be used to trace packet routing on the Internet.

General Troubleshooting

Regardless of problems a network may experience and the solutions to those problems, there is no replacement for prevention on the part of the network administrator. Careful planning and prevention reduce the number of network problems that arise and the downtime to resolve problems that do. An effective network administrator will always perform these general preventative tasks:

Planning

One of the best ways to avoid problems is to carefully plan network administration, implementation, and growth. Plan things that will happen soon in great detail with lots of lists and tables and charts. Plan things that will happen later in less detail, building a foundation for detailed planning later.

Document the current network thoroughly as part of your plan for the future. Plan the logical network, as well as the physical network. Plan for whatever levels of security each part of the network requires. Plan a storage and backup system that deals with the whole network. Plan for fault tolerance and disaster recovery (see the next two chapters).

Standardization

To avoid hardware and software conflicts, network standardization helps reduce potentially difficult and expensive problems. Open standards allow many manufacturers to compete for position in the marketplace and often lead to innovations and growth. Proprietary standards can lock the network into a single vendor, or only a few vendors, limiting your options and your future possibilities.

Documentation

Aside from planning, documentation is the single most important aspect of solving network problems when they occur. Wiring diagrams, notes, and implementation documentation can save network administrators a tremendous amount of time in correcting network problems when they occur. Additionally, careful notes about issues that *could* become problems help solve those problems before they occur.

Network Monitoring

Windows NT Server enables the administrator to monitor the network through various included tools. These tools help the administrator identify problem areas and establish a baseline of acceptable network performance. Network monitoring is discussed in detail in Chapter 19, "Network Monitoring."

For Review

- Tools available to test network traffic issues are DVMs, TDRs, oscilloscopes, advanced cable testers, and Protocol Analyzers.

- TCP/IP utilities such as ping, IPCONFIG, netstat, and tracert help test connectivity and provide general connectivity information.

- Ping early, ping often.

- A Protocol Analyzer measures and logs network traffic at the packet level.

- Digital volt meters can detect open circuits and broken cables.

- Cable breaks can be detected by using one of the following tools:

  Digital volt meter

  Time domain reflectometer

  Advanced cable tester

- Advanced cable testers monitor the overall performance of the network and are able to report problems with a particular cable or network adapter card (NIC) card.

CHAPTER 21

Disaster Recovery

Planning for network disaster recovery is like buying disability income insurance—you fervently hope you never need to use your recovery plan or your disability income insurance. However, if either is ever needed, you'll be much better off if you've planned and prepared for that possible day.

Written Disaster Recovery Plan

External disasters, equipment disasters, and human-mediated disasters all should be in your plan.

1. External disasters

   - Fire

   - Flood

   - Earthquake

   - Lightning

   - Tornado

   - Other natural disasters

   - Power failure

- Transportation failure
- Communication failure

2. Equipment and software disasters
   - Server component failure
   - Network component failure
   - Workstation component failure
   - "Upgrade" software that incapacitates the network

3. Human-mediated disasters
   - Influenza epidemic
   - Sabotage
   - Virus infection

Risk Assessment

Assess all the risks your network is vulnerable to. The items above are only a beginning list to get you started. Then, from the risks you've identified for your network, generate clearly stated precise, prioritized goals for dealing with each risk. These goals and priorities are what will guide you in designing the disaster recovery plan for your network.

Bringing the network back to "business as usual" is often a goal in a disaster recovery plan. What services should come up first? How long are you willing to wait for network services to be back at 100 percent? Should customers be the first to experience "business as usual"? How long before staff will experience "business as usual"? Should physical network-server security be reestablished within 24 hours, or can it wait three days? Should the UNIX servers come up first, or should the Windows NT LAN servers? Should advertising's Macintosh AppleTalk network or parking's support terminals come up last?

TIP

The Networking Essentials exam sometimes has a compound pair of scenario questions involving disaster recovery/file backups. Some people find the wording of the questions to be too complex, so we'll parse the meaning of such questions here. For example, a scenario could call for protecting the network servers from **hardware failure** and preventing downtime **from exceeding two hours**. The optional results call for network virus protection and data access auditing.

If you thought of installing Uninterruptible Power Supplies (UPS) as a possible answer, think again! The requirements are about (1) hardware failure protection and (2) downtime of no more than two hours.

UPS are wonderful tools, and every network should be fully protected by UPS, but UPS do not prevent long downtimes. UPS allow graceful shutdowns. UPS prevent short power failures and brownouts from *becoming* downtime. With a huge amount of overcapacity, an UPS might even prevent *any* downtime in a two-hour failure; however, preventing downtime is still not what the question is asking for!

NOTE: The question also does not say exactly what network services are "down" for two hours, and these details are left to your imagination. Do not waste time figuring out what could have caused a two-hour failure, because it will not help you answer the questions.

So, rethought and reworded, the fault tolerance disaster recovery part of the question is really asking for (1) protection if/when the server hardware fails and (2) fairly rapid data recovery (within two hours).

Now that the question is clearer, what do we have, in the Network Administrator's toolbox, that addresses these two needs?

1. Fault tolerant and redundant hardware designs

2. Data backup systems that can restore all network functions rapidly

So, successful exam candidates look for answers that involve server hardware redundancy and fault tolerance, like RAID (see Chapter 22, "Fault Tolerance"), and backup systems that could conceivably restore the network in under two hours.

This is also one of the two-scenario sets in which you may well figure out the answer to the first item while you work on the second one—look at all scenario-series questions where the question remains the same as opportunities to exercise the teenager's highest skill of *noting differences* between the scenarios. The differences reveal the answers in many MCSE scenario questions.

Also, as mentioned in Chapter 1, "Introduction," notice that if the second scenario *fulfills all the requirements*—then the first scenario probably failed at least one of the optional requirements.

Contingent Resources

These are tough decisions that can involve large amounts of money. Therefore, another part of the disaster recovery plan is to make a thorough hardware and software (licensed and unlicensed) inventory of all network assets, component by component. Also inventory all business insurance covering these assets.

Next, calculate the current network investment. With the current investment figures, you can begin to estimate the resources needed to implement disaster plans under various salvage scenarios. Eventually, management must face the situation and plan to make appropriate contingent resources available in the event of disaster.

Notification Procedures

Your plan should include exact procedures for notification of everyone at the appropriate times. Maintain a comprehensive roster of emergency officials and contacts for all relevant city, county, state, regional, or federal agencies. Murphy's Law says that the one agency or official you leave out will be the one you need the most. Keep this list up-to-date.

Also, you'll possibly need the *home addresses* and *telephone numbers* for:

- Employees crucial to recovery
- Employees affected by the disaster
- Other employees and contractors
- Equipment vendors

Alternate Sites

Many disaster recovery plans require storage of important plan documents and replacement equipment at alternate sites, in the event of a total loss of the primary facility. At the least, duplicate plan documents and backup media must be stored off site. Keeping off-site copies up-to-date must also be a tested part of the plan.

Redundancy at All Points of Failure

Clear responsibilities for every action necessary to implement the plan. It is not enough to designate who is responsible for an action or goal. Be clear about exactly who will perform each activity.

Each responsibility should entail clearly written instructions, checklists, procedures, training requirements, and practice drills to confirm that the person responsible actually can do the task required.

Regular tests of every component of the disaster recovery plan must be built into implementation of the plan. Refine your disaster recovery plan based on the results of these tests, and demand improvements in performance for each testing cycle.

The principle of redundancy also requires that the chain of command be clear, because backup *people* may be required, as well as backup equipment. Who will take over if worker A is unavailable? "Fail-over" responsibilities must be clear, too. Who is responsible to tell worker B to replace worker A if worker A is unavailable?

Back up All Important Data Regularly

Create, implement, enforce, and verify continued performance of a complete, formal backup system, as if your job depended on it. Your job success as an MCSE may well depend on a mundane, boring backup system. When disaster strikes, your ordinary, everyday backups are going to save the company's bacon.

Prioritize the company's data resources. Mission-critical data should receive priority protection. Without data backups to restore everyday data operations, your network's operation, whether it is based on restoration or survival, is irrelevant.

Vital data must be protected with a robust backup system. Ask yourself, can the company afford to start from scratch to replace this data?

A well-designed backup system includes consideration of backup hardware, backup software, backup scheduling, training, tests, and verification. Appropriate replication policies must also be integrated into the backup system.

For Review

Your disaster recovery plan should include:

- A risk assessment
- Contingent resources
- An asset inventory
- Notification procedures
- Alternate sites
- Redundancy at all points of failure

Without a robust backup system for mission-critical data, a disaster recovery plan may be useless.

For Additional Information

Disaster Recovery Links
http://www.alaska.net/~build/DISPLAN.HTM

Network Buyer's Guide—Industry White Papers
http://www.sresearch.com/search/105003.htm

CHAPTER 22

Fault Tolerance

etwork Administrators take steps every day to maintain the integrity of the network's most vital data. By reducing the chances of system failures, you protect critical data and your job.

All computer resources will eventually fail. Some computer parts fail more often than others—nowadays power supplies and hard disk drives fail far too often.

This chapter reviews several practical steps network administrators may take to provide fault tolerance for the network.

Uninterruptable Power Supplies (UPSs)

UPSs are fancy switched batteries. An UPS unit is plugged into the wall alternating current (ac) outlet, and the computer, monitor, and necessary peripherals are then plugged into the UPS. The primary purpose of the UPS is to provide temporary battery power for a graceful shutdown of the computer in the event of a prolonged power failure. An UPS can also prevent the need for shutting down the network by providing power to survive very brief power failures, for example, until regular power is restored by a gasoline-powered generator or through the regular electrical power distribution grid.

A serial connection may connect from the computer and the UPS, to allow the UPS and computer to communicate during a power failure. UPS software is especially designed to control the computer-UPS combination and to enable the graceful shutdown of both devices before the UPS battery is exhausted.

Providing an UPS for a computer also tends to lengthen the computer's useful life by protecting the computer from harmful variations in electrical current. This is because most UPS units also provide line conditioning to smooth over temporary aberrations and spikes in the electrical power supplied to the computer. Although internal computer power supplies originally provided some protection in this regard, today, power supplies manufactured overseas at rock-bottom prices often simply omit these originally designed, but costly, protective features.

Network servers should always be protected with an UPS. Other network devices such as hubs, bridges, and routers can also benefit from UPS protection.

Fault-Tolerant Network Topology

Mesh network topologies have the highest fault tolerance, followed by star topologies. Networks based on bus topologies have the least fault-tolerant design—failure of a single device can bring down the entire network.

Transport media failure, such as cable breaks, have less impact on a mesh topology than on any other topology. Redundant links to all other devices enable data to travel several different paths.

Mesh networks have the advantage of virtually guaranteed communication and are relatively easy to troubleshoot. However, mesh networks are more difficult and expensive to construct, configure, and maintain.

Fault-Tolerant Disk Management

A basic part of planning fault tolerance is planning how to partition your hard disk or disks. Fault-tolerant data systems protect data by duplicating it and by placing it in different physical locations.

Three types of RAID (Redundant Arrays of Inexpensive Disks) are supported by Windows NT Server. They are:

- RAID 0—striping
- RAID 1—mirroring or duplexing
- RAID 5—striping with parity

Of these, only RAID 1 and RAID 5 provide fault tolerance.

RAID 0 is, of course, a misnomer, because there is no redundancy to the data in a RAID 0 striped disk system. For the Networking Essentials exam you should know that RAID 0 means **not fault tolerant.**

Although Windows NT 4.0 supports only RAID Levels 0, 1, and 5, several other levels of RAID exist. See the sidebar for further details.

RAID 0

Disk striping divides data into 64K of RAM blocks and spreads it equally among all disks in the array.

RAID 1

Disk mirroring actually duplicates a partition and places the duplicate onto another physical disk.

Disk duplexing duplicates a partition on another physical disk connected to another hard drive controller.

RAID 5

Disk striping with parity stores data in stripes across multiple drives. Parity sums are calculated and also striped across multiple drives (not a dedicated parity drive). RAID 5 distributes data and parity information across all disks in the array. The data and parity information are always on separate disks. The parity stripe is used for disk reconstruction if a disk fails. Windows NT 4.0 Server supports software RAID 5 with a minimum of 3 disks in the array, and a maximum of 32 disks.

Hardware RAID

The RAID options just described are provided in the Windows NT Server operating system software by Microsoft. RAID hardware cards, particularly those by leading manufacturers such as Adaptec, can provide higher reliability, more fault-tolerant protection, and even greater speed than Microsoft's software solutions. The Internet address URL for Adaptec is given in the resources section at the end of this chapter.

Sector Sparing

On SCSI hard disk drives included in RAID sets, another fault-tolerance technique called *sector sparing* is available. Sector sparing automatically adds sector-recovery capabilities to the file system while the computer is running. During read/write operations, the fault-tolerance disk driver automatically identifies bad sectors and attempts to move data to good sectors and map out (mark as unusable) the bad sectors—a process called *hot fixing*.

Windows NT Disk Administrator

Disk Administrator is a graphical tool for administering disk resources. Figure 22-1 shows the Disk Administrator. It allows you to create or delete partitions and replaces the DOS disk utility. The properties of your hard disks may be changed using Disk Administrator, including changing drive letter assignments, changing a volume label, and formatting the partition. Disk Administrator can also create and manage various disk configurations including mirror sets, stripe sets, stripe sets with parity, and volume sets.

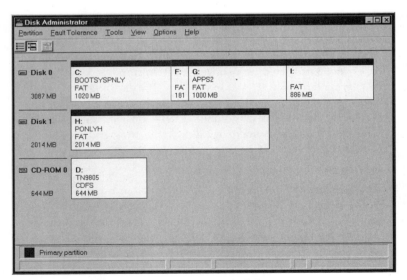

Fig. 22-1. Use Disk Administrator to manage disk resources.

Mirror Set

Mirroring a partition results in automatically creating an exact copy of a partition or disk. This fault-tolerant technique helps ensure that the computer continues to operate, and that you will not lose data. If the primary side of the mirror fails, the system will continue to function from the mirrored side.

Use Disk Administrator to create a mirror set by selecting the two partitions you wish to mirror while holding down the CONTROL key. Select Fault Tolerance / Establish Mirror, as shown in Figure 22-2.

You must format each partition before it is usable, and the mirrored or second portion must be on a different physical disk, must be available (unused) space, and must be the same size.

To boot from the second side of the mirror you must create a "fault-tolerance" boot disk that contains several files: ntldr, ntdetect.com, and boot.ini. You will also need ntbootdd.sys if you are using a SCSI drive without the BIOS enabled. The boot.ini file must reference the mirror partition, so the ARC names must be edited. For example, if your operating system boots from the line

```
multi(0)disk(0)rdisk(0)partition(1)\WINNT="Windows NT Server Version 4.00"
```

you would change it to

```
multi(0)disk(0)rdisk(1)partition(2)\WINNT="Windows NT Server Version 4.00"
```

The first example above refers to the first controller card which is IDE, EIDE, or SCSI with the BIOS enabled [multi(0)], the first

Fig. 22-2. After selecting the two partitions, use Fault Tolerance / Establish Mirror to establish the mirror set.

disk attached to that controller card [rdisk(0)], and the first partition on that disk [partition(1)]. The second entry refers to the first controller, the second disk [rdisk(1)] and the second partition on that disk [partition(2)]. See the sidebar on ARC Naming Conventions for further information.

ARC NAMING CONVENTIONS

ARC (Advanced RISC Computing) naming conventions refer to the method used to identify the path to the operating system you wish to start in the boot.ini file. It consists of four parts:

Multi or *SCSI* refers to the type of controller you are using. Multi refers to an IDE, EIDE, or SCSI adapter with BIOS enabled. SCSI refers to a SCSI adapter without the BIOS enabled. The number contained in the parentheses refers to which controller, with the first one being referred to as 0.

Disk is used if the first entry is SCSI and refers to which hard disk is attached to that controller. Disks are ordinally numbered, so the first disk is 0.

Rdisk is used when the first entry is *multi* and also designates which disk to use. The first disk is referred to as 0.

Partition refers to which partition is on that disk. Partitions are numbered starting with 1, **not** 0.

TIP
Know how to create a boot disk so that you can boot from the second half of your mirror set. See the Microsoft Knowledge Base Article Q119467, "Creating a Boot Disk for an NTFS or FAT Partition," for more information on creating a Windows NT boot disk.

To recover from a failed mirror, replace the failed drive and reboot the computer. Using Disk Administrator, break the mirror by selecting Fault Tolerance/Break Mirror as shown in Figure 22-3. Commit the changes and then create a new mirror set.

Mirroring is a more expensive method of fault tolerance than stripe sets with parity because the amount of available storage on mirrored partitions is cut in half. A conservative strategy is to place only the system and boot files on a mirror set to provide fault tolerance for the most essential parts of your system.

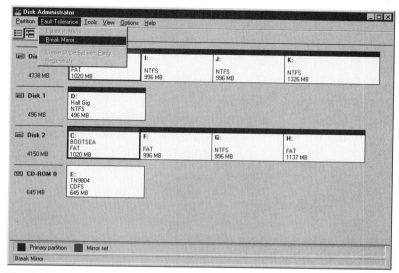

Fig. 22-3. Break the old mirror to begin the process of creating a new mirror.

Microsoft recommends that both disk drives in a mirror set be identical.

> **TIP**
> Disk duplexing is mirroring using two disk controllers rather than one. If one disk controller fails, you can still boot the system. Also, duplexing reads and writes faster than a mirror, because it uses two disk controllers working at the same time.

Stripe sets are faster than mirrors. They are also more economical of disk space than mirrors. System and boot files may be placed on a mirrored partition but not on a stripe set.

> **CAUTION**
> Stripe sets without parity do not provide any fault tolerance. In the case of a disk crash, replace the failed disk, recreate the stripe set, and restore your data from backup.

Stripe Set with Parity

> **TIP**
> Read each question on the exam very carefully. If the question involves a stripe set, never assume that the stripe set is a **stripe set with parity** unless it is stated in the question. Some questions might lead you to

believe that the situation involves a stripe set with parity from the context, but without the words *with parity,* a stripe set is not fault tolerant.

A stripe set with parity consists of 3 to 32 sections of disk space, each of which must be on a separate physical drive, and the whole set appears as one logical drive. Data are written in 64-byte segments sequentially across all the drives as in a stripe set, except that a segment on one disk contains parity information. This information is calculated from the data chunks on that row and the parity information can be used to recover lost data in the case of a single disk failure. See Figure 22-4 for an illustration of how data are written to a stripe set with parity.

The steps for creating a stripe set with parity are similar to creating a stripe set. Select a minimum of three physical disks with free space, up to a maximum of 32 sections; each stripe must be on a separate physical disk. Create the stripe set by selecting Create Stripe Set With Parity from the Fault Tolerance Menu.

TIP
When asked for the largest possible size stripe set, be sure to consider all the different combinations. Don't be taken in by the urge to use space from all available disks. Remember that the size of the stripe set is limited by the smallest available stripe. Combining three large segments of available space might create a larger stripe set than smaller portions of four or five drives.

For Review

- UPS allow for the graceful shutdown of network servers when the power fails.

- A mesh network topology is the most fault tolerant.

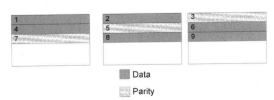

Data
Parity

Fig. 22-4. Data and parity information is written sequentially across a stripe set with parity. Notice that the location of the parity section varies with each stripe.

- RAID 0 is neither redundant nor fault tolerant.
- To be fault tolerant, a stripe set must be a stripe set *with parity.*

For Additional Information

Adaptec: Product Guides and White Papers
  http://www.adaptec.com/products/guide/index.html#wp
Fault-Tolerant Networking
  http://192.215.107.101/nc/netdesign/faultindex.html
NT Fault Tolerance RAID Levels
  http://hma.tierranet.com/nf/mcse/raid.html
Quality Power Supplies and Solid Cases
  http://www.pcpowercooling.com

INDEX

A

Access control, 85–89
  and guest accounts, 95
Access methods, 221–222
Accounts:
  new groups, 197–199
  password policy, 199–200
Accounts Information screen,
  196, 197
Administration, centralized, 96
Advanced cable testers, 252
AppleTalk, 128, 181–182
AppleTalk transaction protocol
  (ATP), 181–182
Application layer, 113
Application servers, 83
ARC (Advanced RISC Comput-
  ing) naming conventions,
  270
ARCnet (Attached Resource
  Computer network), 128,
  167
Asymmetrical Digital Sub-
  scriber Line (ADSL), 64–65
Asynchronous communica-
  tion, 49
Asynchronous Transfer Mode
  (ATM), 65–67
Attenuation, 56, 216–217
  and repeaters, 114

Audio data, 67
Audit Policy, 201–202
AUI connector, 129
Available Bit Rate (ABR), 67
Aviation testing centers, 28

B

Backbones:
  10BaseF for, 165
  10Base5 for, 164
Back end, 82
Backup copies, 204, 263
Bandwidth, 56
Banyan, certificates of, 8
Baseband, 126
Basic rate interface (BRI), 69
Beaconing, 68, 127, 218
Beta tests, 16–18
Binding protocols, 170–171
BNC connectors, 162, 163
Bottlenecks, 219
  causes of, 243
Bridges, 114, 144–149, 223
  broadcasting by, 147, 148
  learning, 146–147
  remote, 148
  versus routers, 152
  source route, 145
  speed buffering, 149

T

TCP/IP (Transmission Control
Protocol/Internet Proto-
col), 170, 172, 177–180
addressing by, 232–235
exam on, 15–16
troubleshooting utilities for,
253–256
TechNet Trial CD, 23
Teleconferencing, 65–66
10BaseF, 165
10Base5, 164–165
10BaseT (twisted-pair Ethernet), 140, 160–161
with no hub, 143
10Base2, 161–163
Terminators, 162, 163
Testing centers, 26–28
checking in, 36–37
ThickNet, 60, 164–165
ThinNet, 59–60, 118, 161–163
troubleshooting, 206–208
Time domain reflector (TDR),
251–252
Token passing, 138, 222
Token Ring frames, 130
Token ring networks, 117–118,
127, 165, 167
and jitter, 220
source route bridging for,
145
Tokens, 127
T1, 71–72
Topologies, network, 50–53,
117–124
Traffic, control solutions,
221–222
Training and Certification News,
21
Transport layer, 112
Transport media, 55–62

Tree network topology, 51, 52
Troubleshooting, 251–258
general, 256–258
TCP/IP utilities for, 253–256
tools of, 251–253
Trusts, 97, 100–102
T3, 72
Twisted-pair cabling, for Ether-
net, 160–161

U

Uninterruptable Power Sup-
plies (UPSs), 261, 265–266
Universal Naming Convention
(UNC), 231–232
UNIX computers, 186
Unshielded twisted-pair (UTP)
cable (IBM Type 3), 58–59
categories of, 58–59
for token ring networks,
167
Unspecified Bit Rate (UBR), 67
User accounts, 192
new, 193–197
User authentication, 99–100
User logon:
single, unified, 96
validation of, 97
User Manager for Domains,
191–202
User productivity, and
domains, 94
User Rights, 201
UTP Ethernet, 160–161

V

Variable Bit Rate (VBR), 67
Video data, 67

ABOUT THE AUTHORS

Dave Kinnaman, MCSE, a writer in Austin, Texas, has co-authored many books and articles about computers and the Internet. Dave is particularly involved in information access issues, including Internet filtering software, disability access, and retirement issues on the Internet.

LouAnn Ballew, MCSE, is a networking consultant with 17 years in the computer industry. Her interests include online research methodology, doctor-patient and patient-patient communication issues caused by the current health care system, and relocation to the Pacific Northwest.